D0205600

Elizabeth Bowen

Revised Edition

Twayne's English Authors Series

Kinley E. Roby, Editor

Northeastern University

TEAS 123

ELIZABETH BOWEN
(1899–1973)
Photograph by Angus MacBean. Courtesy of Jonathan Cape Ltd.

Elizabeth Bowen

Revised Edition

By Allan E. Austin

University of Guelph

Twayne Publishers
A Division of G. K. Hall & Co. • Boston

Elizabeth Bowen, Revised Edition
Allan E. Austin

Published by Twayne Publishers
A Division of G. K. Hall & Co.
70 Lincoln Street
Boston, Massachusetts 02111

Copyediting supervised by Barbara Sutton
Book production by Janet Zietowski-Reynolds
Book design by Barbara Anderson

Typeset in 11 pt. Garamond
by Compositors Typesetters of Cedar Rapids, Iowa

Printed on permanent/durable acid-free paper
and bound in the United States of America

Library of Congress Cataloging-in-Publication Data
Austin, Allan E.
Elizabeth Bowen / by Allan E. Austin,—Rev. ed.
p. cm.—(Twayne's English authors series ; TEAS 123)
Bibliography: p.
Includes index.
ISBN 0-8057-6972-2 (alk. paper)
1. Bowen, Elizabeth, 1899–1973—Criticism and interpretation.
I. Title. II. Series.
PR6003.06757Z57 1989
823'.912—dc19 88-24502
CIP

Contents

About the Author

Allan E. Austin received his B.A. from Michigan State University (magna cum laude) and his M.A. and a Ph.D. from the University of Rochester. He has taught at the University of Rochester, Russell Sage College, and, since 1965, at the University of Guelph, Guelph, Ontario, where he is an associate professor and teaches courses in twentieth-century British literature.

Dr. Austin is the author of *Roy Fuller* in Twayne's English Authors Series. He also wrote the chapter on Roy Fuller in the Dictionary of Literary Biography volume, *British Poets 1914–1945*. His most recent work has been on Anthony Powell's *A Dance to the Music of Time*, and he reviews frequently. He is also a noted Canadian watercolorist.

Preface

The last decade has been especially gratifying for admirers of Elizabeth Bowen. Victoria Glendinning's splendid biography, *Elizabeth Bowen, Portrait of a Writer,* stimulated renewed interest in 1977 and was followed by Hermoine Lee's detailed critical study, *Elizabeth Bowen: An Estimation* (1981). But these are merely the high points in the steady critical conversation prompted by the creations of this urbane stylist and thoughtful and witty observer of life in her time. As well, we have had a sensitive British television production of *The Death of the Heart* (1986). Meanwhile paperback publishers continue to make available a substantial portion of the author's work that appropriately allows for her inclusion in college literature courses.

Certainly one of the aims of this study when it first appeared in 1971 was to urge the merit of Bowen. Now this no longer appears so pressing a concern: Elizabeth Bowen can be seen as one of the elect of significant twentieth-century British authors. Critics continue to debate whether her place is of a particular time—the thirties and forties—or timeless, and to consider the relative merit of her best novels vis-à-vis her best short stories, but these are matters of a different order.

It is now timely, then, to update this book. This volume addresses the reader who is likely encountering Elizabeth Bowen for the first time (and, based on personal observation, who may well be a student writing a paper on one of Bowen's novels or stories). This aims to provide a succinct introduction to the author's most important work, her fiction. Other studies, especially Hermoine Lee's, also consider Bowen's extensive body of nonfiction. Three of the six chapters are new: chapter 1, a brief biography and general consideration of Bowen's chief concerns and style; chapter 5, an examination of the best of the shorter fiction; and chapter 6, a brief survey of critical discussion. The remaining three chapters, on the novels, reflect minor revision. These latter chapters are mainly informed summaries of the novels and are intended to provide the Bowen novice with a convenient means of placing whatever has been read in the full novelistic context. These summaries, the reader will appreciate, are but roadmaps of a vital literary landscape.

Allan E. Austin

University of Guelph

Acknowledgments

To Kinley E. Robey, editor, and to Barbara Sutton, manuscript editor, I want to express appreciation for thoughtful assistance.

The photograph of Elizabeth Bowen is by Angus MacBean, and was provided by Jonathan Cape Ltd., London.

Chronology

1899	Elizabeth Bowen born 7 June in Dublin.
1906	Settles in England with mother following father's illness.
1912	Mother dies.
1914–1917	Attends Downe House School, Downe, Kent.
1918	Attends London County Council School of Art.
1923	*Encounters;* marries Alan Charles Cameron; living in Headington, Oxford.
1926	*Ann Lee's.*
1927	*The Hotel.*
1929	*Joining Charles; The Last September.*
1930	Father dies; inherits Bowen's Court, County Cork.
1931	*Friends and Relations.*
1932	*To the North.*
1934	*The Cat Jumps.*
1935	*The House in Paris;* moves to Clarence Terrace, Regent's Park, London, when husband joins the BBC.
1938	*The Death of the Heart.*
1939–1945	Stays in London during World War II working as an air-raid warden and for the Ministry of Information; home badly damaged in bombing.
1941	*Look at All Those Roses.*
1942	*Bowen's Court.*
1945	*The Demon Lover* (published in the United States as *Ivy Gripped the Steps*).
1948	Made a Commander of the British Empire.
1949	*The Heat of the Day*; receives honorary doctor of letters, Trinity College, Dublin.
1950	*Collected Impressions.*
1952	Moves to Bowen's Court; Alan Cameron dies.

1955 *A World of Love.*

1957 Receives honorary doctor of letters, Oxford University.

1960 Sells Bowen's Court and returns to Old Headington.

1962 *Afterthoughts.*

1964 *The Little Girls.*

1965 *A Day in the Dark;* moves to Hythe, Kent; made a Companion of Literature.

1969 *Eva Trout.*

1973 Dies 22 February in London.

Chapter One

The Bowen World

Poised, detached, witty, and regal in the face of uncertainty and in the assured knowledge of the abyss, this, quintessentially, is the story of Elizabeth Bowen *and* Elizabeth Bowen's story. A kingdomless aristocrat dedicated to high standards, but clear-eyed and tough-mindedly committed to making an art of life and a life of art, Elizabeth Bowen achieved remarkable distinction in both.

Biography in Brief

Elizabeth Dorothea Cole Bowen was born in Dublin on 7 June 1899. Her parents, Henry Cole and Florence Colley Bowen, were Anglo-Irish. The family estate, Bowen's Court, near Kildorrey, County Cork, was built in the eighteenth century by Colonel Henry Bowen, who acquired the land through coming to Ireland in 1749 in the service of Oliver Cromwell. By the time of Elizabeth's childhood the position of the Anglo-Irish was becoming increasingly precarious. To be Anglo-Irish may imply one is both English and Irish; the nearer reality is, one is not quite either. In later years Elizabeth Bowen suggested she was most at home in the middle of the Irish Sea.[1] Though she lived most of her life in England, Elizabeth Bowen's heart was closest to Ireland.

As privileged Protestant inhabitants of big houses (not nearly so big as their English counterparts) and their outlying demesnes in a poor Roman Catholic country longing for independence, the Anglo-Irish were the objects of both regard and disdain. Although Bowen's Court, unlike so many such houses, was never burned, the possibility long haunted Elizabeth Bowen. For these landlords, survival virtually dictated an unusual sensibility: to never quite register one's position, to never really acknowledge the pressure of guilt, to carry on as if the inevitable future and the nighttime fire terror did not exist. This regal ability of seeming not to notice, of being able to look through or past difficulties, of maintaining an illusion of normalcy became an art for Elizabeth Bowen.

Elizabeth's earliest years were divided between summers at Bowen's Court and winters in Dublin where her father was a barrister. Surrounded by relatives, the Bowens were socially active, but normal family life came to an abrupt end when she was seven. Henry Bowen suffered a nervous breakdown—Bowen's Court doubtless one of its causes—and was institutionalized. He subsequently recovered to resume his career, although never again with his family at his side. Elizabeth moved to England with her mother and embarked on a lengthy period of transience. For the first few years they lived in various communities on the coast of Kent. Florence Bowen was a fey woman, somewhat remote from life and inclined to the impractical. Nevertheless she and Elizabeth—known in her childhood as "Bitha"—were very close. When Elizabeth was thirteen Florence became ill with cancer. The pretense that had become part of their lives now really flourished. Henry arrived, and amid the talk of Florence's recovery was the planning to return reunited to Bowen's Court. Elizabeth knew it was all fabrication. Shortly thereafter Florence died, and Henry was back in Dublin. In the years following Elizabeth lived with different English relatives. From 1914 until the summer of 1917 she attended Downe House School near Orpington, Kent. Here in perhaps the happiest period of her growing years she found companionship, became well regarded, and enjoyed the friendship of the headmistress, Olive Willis, who in later years was able to provide a timely assist to her career as a budding writer.

The shocks and dislocations of these early years disclosed Elizabeth's resources of poised bravado. Her decision to begin writing is an aspect of this. She has written, "All through my youth I lived with a submerged fear that I might fail to establish a grown-up status. . . . A writer and a grown-up, it appeared to me, could not but be synonymous."[2] She began writing stories when she was twenty and first publication followed two years later.

In 1923, while living in Oxford, Elizabeth met and shortly married Alan Charles Cameron, the Secretary for Education for the Oxford school system. The marriage proved a happy and lasting one, although a puzzling one for many of Bowen's subsequent friends and acquaintances. Some suspect it was never consummated. Cameron seemed unsuited to Bowen's flourishing social life, and the image in *The Death of the Heart* of Thomas Quayne sitting alone in his study while his wife Anna entertains her men friends in the drawing room above apparently has its basis in truth. Yet Elizabeth was intensely loyal to her husband and would brook no criticism of him. The Camerons lived in the Oxford suburb of Old Headington for ten years before Alan joined the BBC in 1935, at which time they moved to London and a lovely home overlooking Regent's Park.

Once Bowen's first book appeared, a collection of short stories in the same year as her marriage, her writing career developed steadily to the accompaniment of growing critical recognition. She was particularly fecund when it came to producing reviews and articles in addition to her stories and novels. She was a popular hostess who thrived in a vital intellectual milieu that did not readily suffer dullards. Socially she mingled with members of the Bloomsbury set and counted T. S. Eliot and his wife, Vivien, as friends. There were love affairs. She reached the zenith of her romantic life in the years immediately before and during World War II with Charles Ritchie, a Canadian diplomat stationed in London. This open relationship flourished with Cameron's apparent approbation.

Elizabeth made regular journeys to Bowen's Court, especially after she inherited it in 1930. It was the scene of frequent summer entertaining. Her attachment and loyalty to Ireland and the Irish never wavered. During the war the British government sent her to Ireland to prepare a report on the mood and attitudes of the Irish. The Camerons remained in London throughout the war, and Elizabeth, who served for a time as an AR warden, said it was the most interesting period of her life. Certainly it inspired some of her best fiction. Perhaps it was in keeping with so many facets of her life that her Regent's Park home was badly damaged in the bombing.

After the war Cameron's health began to decline. He resigned from his position, and it was decided they would spend more time in Ireland. By now Ritchie was married and back in Canada. The great times were over. When Cameron died in 1952 Elizabeth decided to remain permanently at Bowen's Court. She began spending considerable periods in the United States as a lecturer and writer-in-residence at a variety of universities; these experiences she greatly enjoyed. The upkeep of Bowen's Court eventually became so burdensome that she sold it in 1960 to a man who tore it down shortly thereafter.

The closing phase of Bowen's life rather recapitulated earlier times. For a period she lived again in Old Headington, then bought a house in Hythe, Kent. She finally settled again in London, where, like her mother, she died of cancer, in February 1973 with Charles Ritchie at her bedside.

Elizabeth Bowen was not beautiful but distinguished looking, tall and regal in bearing. Admiring grace and style she achieved both in her personal life and in her writing. As friends have noted, she was one who enhanced and enlarged life. An early Oxford friend, the distinguished classics scholar C. M. Bowra, wrote of her:

> She was tall and very well built and had the manners of someone who has lived in the country and knows its habits. She was handsome in an unusual way, with a face that indicated both mind and character. Unlike some Irish, she did not talk for effect but

kept the conversation at a high level and gave her full attention to it. She had a slight stutter which added force to her remarks. She had the fine style of a great lady, who on rare occasions was not shy of slapping down impertinence, but she came from a society where the decorum of the nineteenth century had been tempered by an Irish frankness. With all her sensibility and imagination, she had a masculine intelligence which was fully at home in large subjects and general ideas, and when she sometimes gave a lecture, it was delivered with a force and control of which most University teachers would be envious. Though she was entirely at home in the modern world and deeply committed to it, she had her roots in a more spacious and more assured society.[3]

Victoria Glendinning objects to Bowra's use of the word *stutter*: "It was a stammer, not a stutter—she was very particular about the distinction."[4] This hesitation over certain words, typically, did not deter her from frequent appearances on BBC radio programs or inhibit her university work. She was largely able to command it, but in any event it was looked upon as an endearing characteristic. Clearly her life and career mark Elizabeth Bowen as a remarkable, courageous, and energetic person as her fiction marks her as intelligent, witty, and aesthetically stylish.

The ten novels and more than eighty short stories Bowen wrote are only part of her impressive productivity. Her work for newspapers and magazines was voluminous. Many of her articles, reviews, prefaces, and radio talks were collected in two volumes, *Afterthoughts* and *Collected Impressions*. In addition to the story of her family history, *Bowen's Court*, she wrote *Seven Winters*, a recollection of the Dublin of her childhood years; *Castle Anna*, a play concerning an Irish big house; *A Time in Rome*, a very personal record of her feelings about this city; and *The Good Tiger*, a story for children.

The Realm of Concern

Though conveying a strong sense of the mood and feel of life in England (and to a lesser extent of Ireland) in the thirties and forties, Elizabeth Bowen's fiction, at its best, transcends any historical dimension by its striking and provocative treatment of timeless experience. The author is fascinated by the journey of youth to adulthood with all its attendant hazards; by the interaction between youth, with its still romantically charged will and expectations, and adulthood, with, more often than not, its withdrawal behind social shields covering disenchantment consequent upon betrayal, loss, and change; by the individual's challenging struggle to attain self-realization and vital rapport with society. As these archetypal concerns are translated into fiction they are readily enhanced by being placed in a fully realized context and by being filtered through the complex vision of the authorial narrator.

Elizabeth Bowen's characters find the confusions and deprivations of their times especially inimical to the working out of their fates. The author approaches the present as a conservative whose ideal is the big Irish country house. Although it spells out this ideal, her study of her family history, *Bowen's Court*, is actually a lament for its passing. The tearing down of Bowen's Court, recorded at the end of the book, is sadly emblematic. The big house with its demesne and obligations gave its possessors a stabilizing center and purpose. Imposing the traditional duties of the past, its present concerns also recognized obligations to the future. As an embodiment of responsibility, style, and community, the big house was something to live up to. This conception, generally more felt than expressed, is in the fiction the means of measuring the follies and failures of the contemporary English middle class.

The present is a disconcerting place. For Elizabeth Bowen, "Our century, as it takes its frantic course, seems barely habitable by humans."[5] In the face of rapid change, rampantly competing wills, and rage for immediate gratification, values have blurred into confusion. The author observes that "The decline of manners in the grand and fixed sense has made behaviour infinitely more difficult."[6] The forces of modern barbarism have virtually laid siege to those of civility. To Bowen, World War II seemed to follow logically as a doom foretold.

The correlation between the turbulent times and the author's formative experiences is evident: it is hardly surprising that the world appeared uncertain and threatening to one whose normal family life was shattered at seven, who was thirteen when her mother suddenly died, who expected the family estate to be burned to the ground on any given night, and whose elegant London home was blasted by bombs. Dislocation, the operative norm, was what had to be faced. In Bowen's view all fiction is "transposed autobiography," though probably so removed "as to defeat ordinary recognition."[7] On the whole her work reflects her own times and centers on women making their way precariously across the minefield of life. The odds favoring their surviving relatively unscathed are never high.

The energy of human desire assures drama, since the ego and will of the individual is inevitably on a collision course with conditions and with other egos that are frequently stronger and more worldly. A young woman in "The Disinherited" thinks, "One is empowered to live fully: occasion does not offer." In "A Summer Night," the heroine, Emma, arranges a night away from a husband who does not understand her needs in order to keep an assignation. As she drives cross country the mellow evening and lush Irish countryside reinforce her mounting sense of enchantment, but it takes very little time for her pragmatic lover to deflate this. Recurringly Bowen's fiction explores the desire-driven protagonist's exposure and reaction to the unexpected; a salient constituent is the motif of a journey that registers the shift from place to displacement. Taken as a whole, Bowen's work displays a remarkable inventiveness in playing variations of this basic situation. Her range of moods is extensive, sometimes light, often dark, frequently a blending since she perceives the distance between the comedy of manners and personal tragedy as slight.

"The Working Party." Most of the characteristics I have been noting can be observed in "The Working Party," a relatively simple story that also nicely displays the author's ability to draw the reader into her tongue-in-cheek embrace. Mrs. Fisk, a new bride at twenty-one and largely unformed, is egotistical, complacent, and willful. For the first time she is to entertain the local sewing circle in her large farm home. She is determined that her party will be surpassing, and her preparations are elaborate. On the afternoon of the gathering her husband and his men are working in a distant field so "she and the Working Party are to be absolutely alone." As the ladies begin arriving Mrs. Fisk finds herself pulled between "apprehension and pleasure." Here, then, is the idealizing and presumptuous protagonist, ripe for exposure to some disruptive shock-administering counter force since this is the way of the world. She receives cautionary forewarning. When some of the ladies recall the difficulties of their hostess's deceased mother-in-law, Mrs. Fisk tosses her chin and says, "*I've* had no difficulties." The vicar's wife assures her she is most fortunate, "and her tone [says]: 'That is not the lot of the human soul . . . that is not the lot of woman'."[8]

The attack on Mrs. Fisk arrives in the form of a dead body. Going down the short flight of back stairs leading to the kitchen, she finds Cottesby the cowherd slumped there. This occurrence is not entirely unexpected, since the man has had "a heart" for years. Still, Mrs. Fisk's chilly response, "What of it?," is disconcerting. While unsettled, her determination to make the party a success stiffens her and the fact that Phyllis the cook is crying and neglecting her duties simply bolsters the sense that "nothing should wreck her." This willful, immediate reaction is not the telling one. What Mrs. Fisk in her unpreparedness cannot foresee is the force that unacknowledged fear and guilt will exert upon her imagination. When the vicar's wife subsequently wonders if Mrs. Fisk still has her mother-in-law's beautiful copper preserving pans, Mrs. Fisk begins to picture the vicar's wife "walking about the house . . . opening and shutting doors." Suddenly she imagines the ladies laying out Cottesby on her kitchen table. Then she is recalled to reality by the empty tea urn: the plans for Phyllis to appear with more hot water have gone awry.

The final action, "the journey," follows. A shaken Mrs. Fisk rises to fetch the water, maintaining her composure until she quits her parlor but finding she cannot bring herself to go down the stairs again past the dead man. Quitting the house she flees across the fields seeking her husband. The story wryly concludes, "She had forgotten the Working Party." Mrs. Fisk's experience is doubtless salutary, unsettling but not damaging. In stories involving the deeper commitment of love, however, the consequences are correspondingly radical.

What Bowen's more serious works have in common with "The Working Party" is the inevitability, willingly or otherwise, of the heroine's unsettlement. Some long to escape their milieux (like Lois in *The Last September* and Karen in *The House in Paris*), or to change it (like Janet in *Friends and Relations*), or to preserve a threatened status quo even though it may be moribund or corrupt (like Anna in *The Death of the Heart* and Stella in *The Heat of the Day*). Unsettlement, naturally, is an ambivalent matter; but initially it must be seen as the basis of reality. Expulsion from Eden is the beginning of selfhood and wisdom. Bowen knows that "this struggle for life, a struggle that goes on everywhere, that may be said in fact, to be *life* itself . . . should not therefore have anything terrible about it."[9] What so many of the protagonists, having been jolted into awareness, must decide is, in the words of Robert Frost, "What to make of a diminished thing".[10] The author implicitly provides an answer.

The specific inner dramas of the novels and stories have their particular meanings, but the essential significance of Bowen's work resides in the outer, enveloping vision of the authorial narrator. This becomes the metaphysical counterpart to the big house ideal. In actual circumstances the author could not control the fate of Bowen's Court; she can determine her way of viewing and responding to the world. Her persona has much in common with that of Alexander Pope in *The Rape of the Lock*, where worldly wit and good will temper cool, ironic observation. Victoria Glendinning identifies two distinct impulses to which Elizabeth Bowen is inclined. One is toward an "almost vulgar gypsy romanticism" and the other toward "perfect ladylike demeanour and beautiful manners."[11] The drive to fuse these into a unified vision clearly fuelled her creativity.

Bowen's work is particularly satisfying because her concerns are viewed with complexity and expressed in an attractive, urbane style. Nothing being simple, the primary act is to recognize this. The unknowableness of human motivation is fascinating but means that many stories must conclude with "a querry: exactly what happened next (or, in some cases, exactly what *had* happened) is left to the reader to conjecture."[12] Regardless of circumstance, in the end Elizabeth Bowen shares a viewpoint expressed by her contemporary W. H. Auden in such lines as, "Life remains a blessing," and "Find our mortal world enough."[13]

The Realm of Realization

Elizabeth Bowen is one of this century's most distinguished British stylists. Her vision of life in her times emerges from a forceful fusion of inner tension and outer urbanity. In critical discussions of her literary affinities no one is more astute than Walter Allen in seeing her as a unique blending of Jane Austen and Henry James.[14] This is a most appropriate and distinguished parentage for a writer whose keynote is duality. On the Austen side, with a nod as well to E. M. Forster, is the concern for the English middle classes, the penetrating satire they elicit and the ever-present sense of worldly humor and goodwill. On the James side is the psychological concern for the darker sides of human motivation, the possibilities of inner haunting or fantasy, the importance of saving illusion, the connotative use of locale, the linking of the aesthetic and the moral, and the mandarin approach to language. Tension characterizes Bowen's work.

The quintessential activity in Bowen's fiction is worry. On the whole her characters reflect unease, uncertainty, puzzlement, and wariness. They inhabit a world of nervosity. The minds of her principal characters chew away relentlessly on their immediate morsels of concern. Here is an example from the opening chapter of *The Heat of the Day*, where an as yet unidentified man is sitting hunched over on a bench in Regent's Park:

> The futility of the heated inner speed, the alternate racing to nowhere and coming to dead stops, made him guy himself. Never yet had he not got *somewhere*. By casting about—but then hitherto this had always been done calmly—he had never yet not come on a policy which both satisfied him and in the end worked. There never had yet not been a way through, a way round or, in default of all else, a way out. But in this case he was thinking about a woman.[15]

The syntactical contortions convey the underlying pressures and capture the uncertainty operating at the cutting edge of unfolding experience.

As a rule the author engages in five activities: evoking locale or ambience; describing action; recording the dialogue of her characters; suggesting their inner thoughts, feelings, or responses; and providing authorial comment. In practice, of course, these activities may alternate and several of them merge in a particular passage.

Bowen has a particular gift for realizing sense of place and ambience. Never simply a stage or backdrop for action, locale is an integral feature of her work. For her, time and place "are more than elements, they are actors."[16] Especially sensitive to place, she reports that a work may have its origins in a particular setting: reified by certain lighting and atmospherics, a setting can evoke potent moods and feelings that challenge the writer's imagination to provide appropriate characters and situations to fulfill the sense of dramatic potential. Many of the novels and stories commence with suggestive descriptions of place that both establish the desired context and anticipate the direction or destination of the narrative.

One of Bowen's most widely admired accomplishments was her depiction of the appearance and feel of London under the siege of bombing during World War II in *The Heat of the Day* and *The Demon Lover and Other Stories*. From an artistic viewpoint, the intersection of the blitz and the author was fortuitous as this representative passage from *The Heat of the Day* suggests:

> In reality there were no holidays; few were free however light-headedly to wander. The night behind and the night to come met across every noon in an arch of strain. To work or to think was to ache. In offices, factories, ministries, shops, kitchens the hot yellow sands of each afternoon ran out slowly; fatigue was the one reality. You dared not envisage sleep. Apathetic, the injured and dying in the hospitals watched light change on walls which might fall tonight. Those rendered homeless sat where they had been sent; or, worse, with the obstinancy of animals retraced their steps to look for what was no longer there. Most of all the dead, from mortuaries, from under cataracts of rubble, made their anonymous presence—not as today's dead but as yesterday's living—felt through London. Uncounted, they continued to move in shoals through the city day, pervading everything to be seen or heard or felt with their torn-off senses, drawing on this tomorrow they had expected—for death cannot be so sudden as all that. (86)

The reader familiar with Bowen's typical interests will appreciate how readily she responded to these exacerbating circumstances, but seeping through the registration of the strain and horror is the artist's creative exuberance.

Homes assume major roles in much of Bowen's work. The very title of *The House in Paris* points the way to this and is in no sense atypical. Homes are integral to the meaning and working out of many stories as a reading of, for example, *The Last September*, "Ivy Gripped the Steps," "The Demon Lover," "The Disinherited," and "The Cat Jumped" disclose. Very often the author will contrast homes as a means of mutual illumination and moral clarification. In *The Death of the Heart*, 2, Windsor Terrace is juxtaposed to "Waikiki," as is Holme Dene to Montford in *The Heat of the Day*. What lingers in the afterglow of such stories as "A Day in the Dark" and "No. 16" are the disturbing settings.

In a sense Bowen's fiction is always developing and sustaining ambience. While much of this activity can be isolated in blocks of description, like the citation from *The Heat of the Day*, there is always incidental input mingling with other practices. This illustrative paragraph from "The Disinherited" shows the author rapidly yet seamlessly melding several activities; for in addition to sustaining an already established sense of decadence, she presents action, reveals inner feeling, offers an authorial comment, and includes, albeit briefly, dialogue:

> He turned back into his room, and Davina, with automatic swiftness and energy, went springing upstairs after him. His door stayed ajar; vibrations of heat from the stove came down through the arch to the horrified Marianne. Looking up at the dark sky, she fought for a feeling of everybody's nonentity. The clock in the church tower, not far away, struck nine: before the last stroke finished Davina was down again. She caught Marianne by the elbow and ran her across the yard. They paused by the lamp a minute; Davina held a crackling note close up to Marianne's face. "That is that," she said.[17]

The appropriate term for Bowen's self-conscious poetic use of language is impressionistic. Calculated to reverberate, the prose nicely conveys the ambiguities and imponderables of experience that underscore her vision.[18] In approaching her material as more of an X-ray than a camera, she projects essences. It is work calling for sensitive and intelligent reading. Bowen is conscious of her call for collaboration: "In so far as the writer has known more than he says, the reader will in his turn draw from the pages more than is there in print."[19] As she recognizes, it is a process requiring time: "The work of imagination causes a long, reflective halt in the reader's faculties. It demands to be reread, to be brooded over, to be ingested, to be lived with and *in*."[20]

If it is true that all human beings respond to experience primarily in one of two ways, either by mental or by emotional comprehension initially, then Bowen is one of the latter. She has a predilection for feeling over seeing and for reaction rather than action as this passage indicates:

> The experience which really influences art does not consist in drama or incidents; it is a sort of emotional accumulation, or, at its best, a slowly-acquired deep-down knowledge. Experience is the reaction to what happens, not to the happening itself—and in that sense experience is, like environment, to a degree selected. The meaning

which is extracted from occurrence varies and varies in its importance, according to the writer's choice as to feeling: he allows some things to "take" with him more than others.[21]

One of the challenges Bowen's reader must face is the constantly altering flow of emotional currents.

Dialogue is both prominent and important. Bowen exploits its potential for suggestiveness and allusiveness and finds it a natural arena of tension where the serious gamesmanship of social intercourse occurs. Artistically, dialogue is the ideal provenance for the dangerous and hence dramatic mixing of explicitness and reticence, of duplicity and incomprehension. Naturally she favors the oblique over the direct and exploits the natural ellipses of conversation. Bowen is fond of focusing on the impact conversation or a monologue makes upon an auditor and may intermingle dialogue and the listener's response.

Certainly one of the most attractive features in this work is the presence of the authorial narrator who emerges as an ideal human being, perceptive, fair, wise, and condemnatory when need be, humorous, and wise. The aperçus, such as this one from *The Death of the Heart*, are a dividend:

But a man must live! Not for nothing do we invest so much of ourselves in other people's lives—or even in momentary pictures of people we do not know. It cuts both ways: the happy group inside the lighted window, the figure in the long grass in the orchard seen from the train stay and support us in our dark hours. Illusions are art, for the feeling person, and it is by art that we live, if we do. It is the emotion to which we remain faithful, after all: we are taught to recover it in some other place.[22]

This authorial presence serves numerous purposes: perhaps pulling the reader back from the immediate scene in the interest of a broader perspective, or showing the way to compassion or accommodation, or possibly drawing a surprising though apt conclusion from events. Occasionally the narrator enjoys a comic turn. Here is a delightful instance from *To the North*, where at issue is the most suitable bus from which an unaccompanied child might explore London:

she had asked Mrs. Patrick, the housekeeper, if it would be suitable for a young girl of her age to go out alone for a ride in a bus. (Pauline had been told what happens in London and warned, especially, to avoid hospital nurses.) Mrs. Patrick, with hospital nurses also in mind, said it depended entirely upon the character of the bus. Taking thought, she had recommended the No. 11. The No. 11 is an entirely moral bus. Springing from Shepher's Bush, against which one has seldom heard anything, it en-

> joys some innocent bohemianism in Chelsea, picks up the shoppers at Peter Jones's, swerves down the Pimlico Road—too busy to be lascivious—passes not too far from the royal stables, nods to Victoria Station, Westminster Abbey, the Houses of Parliament, whirrs reverently up Whitehall, and from its only brush with vice, in the Strand, plunges to Liverpool Street through the noble and serious architecture of the City. Except for the Strand, the No. 11 route, Mrs. Patrick considered, had the quality of a Sunday afternoon literature; from it Pauline could derive nothing but edification.[23]

Actually the fiction offers a considerable range of humor from subtle irony to the flamboyantly grotesque.

In her personal life Elizabeth Bowen displayed exemplary style and vivacity. These same characteristics mark her fiction. A thoughtful observer and a dedicated craftsman, she provides an amplitude of entertainment, insight, wisdom, and aesthetic pleasure.

Chapter Two

The Sleeping Beauties

Violence is born of the
desire to escape oneself.

—Iris Murdoch, *The Bell*

Elizabeth Bowen's ten novels may be conveniently divided into three groups because of their central concerns. The division, with one deviation the natural chronology, is: 1) her first, second, and fourth novels; 2) her third, fifth, and sixth; and 3) her final four.

What *The Hotel* (1927), *The Last September* (1929), and *To the North* (1932) share is a young heroine either experiencing "serious" love or on the verge of doing so. In each case the woman is attractive and intelligent but emotionally unprepared for the situations in which she finds herself or provokes. When not one of the novels culminates in love, let alone marriage, we have an indication of what the novel of manners has become in the context of this disoriented century. The girls in *The Hotel* and in *The Last September* are left "free" at the close of the novel, but they are undoubtedly wiser about themselves and the ways of the world, and they are presumably in a position to meet the male sex in reasonable and authentic terms. The heroine of *To the North* finds a solution to her problems in death.

These books provide a neat progression in their respective relationships between narrative and environment: on the one hand, they move from the most artificial to the most normative milieu; on the other, from the least to the most dramatic or radical story. Thus, *The Hotel* is light in tone; *To the North*, dark. *The Last September* is the most personal, nostalgic, and mellow of Bowen's works.

As well, these novels present an interesting study in variation. Each story revolves about a "dark" character whose true nature for one reason or another is not readily discernible, and the narrative concludes when this person is illuminated. In *The Hotel*, Sydney's problem is to come to terms, in her own mind, with the figure of Mrs. Kerr; in *The Last September*, Lois must come to see herself. In each novel, visual recognition may in each case be considered as a sign of growth and as a talisman of reasonable expectation. Emmeline's situation in *To the North* is somewhat apart, for she is the mystery in her novel. Her only chance for survival resides in her being seen by someone else before catastrophe strikes; this just fails to happen. The novel's final situation is starkly ironic, for the one person who suddenly understands her is the man who, from her viewpoint, betrayed her; but he sees too late and must pay for his tardiness with his life. Bowen's problem in *To the North* involves the reader directly as the other two novels do not; for the reader, like her lover, cannot see Emmeline until the close, which means Miss Bowen must marshall the characterization of her heroine in such a way as to sustain her mystery.

If *To the North* is more successful in individual scenes than in toto, the failure may lie less in the author's execution than in the basic premise that such a problem can yield a successful artistic solution. Bowen's chief aim is to keep Emmeline off stage as much as possible; thus, a considerable amount of talk about her ensues on the part of other characters. Accordingly, this limits the meaningful kind of subjective interplay between sparring individuals, which is normally one of the chief delights of a Bowen novel. The book is not without such exchanges, principally between Emmeline and the most interesting of the characters, Markie; but these are minimal. Furthermore, the author employs a mirrorlike subplot involving the child, Pauline. These scenes, in themselves pleasing, are heavy-handed insofar as the main story is concerned. The two plots are secured through parallels and contrasts between Emmeline and Pauline, but these prove less than satisfactory because they are so blatant. So, again, the author places herself in a position in which she must forego another of her keenest attributes—subtlety.

Still, whatever its flaws, *To the North* remains a more impressive novel than the author's first, *The Hotel*. Her fourth novel has, as indeed it should, a scenic force and a control absent from the initial one. To begin with, a writer who assembles a cast in a calculated manner and who employs the confines of, say, a boat, an army platoon, or a hotel immediately acquires added artistic obligations. Despite the seeming complexity created by a disparate collection of individuals and by a temporary context, the reader suspects the author of actually setting up an easy problem capable of dramatic but ultimately of simple resolution. Bowen does not really displace these built-in expectations. In her best work the reader's paramount interest arises not from "what will happen?" but from "why is this happening?" *The Hotel* is largely concerned with the first question.

The Hotel has strong affinities with Jane Austen's *Emma*. In each book the heroine overestimates her capabilities, and therein resides the motivation for action; each engages in creating pitfalls for herself. *But* there are two immediate differences between the novels. Austen creates in Emma a rich character whom the reader may simultaneously laugh at and love; Bowen offers in Sydney a heroine neither likable nor really corporeal and therefore hardly engaging. Again, part of the force of *Emma* results from the closed world in which the characters reside, which means, painfully and deliciously, they must, no matter what transpires, go on living together. *The Hotel* presents an open world, and the tentative nature of the character configurations drain away a great deal of dramatic pressure. The youthful Elizabeth Bowen, who was too ambitious and injudicious with this effort, created among others, the problem of choreographing for an extensive cast. That she manages to do so as well as she does should have been ample forewarning at the time of her future accomplishment. She went on to follow Thoreau's wise counsel, "Simplify, simplify"; and, in due course, she accomplishes much more with much less.

The Last September, the first of the successful novels, skillfully integrates a number of fine characterizations, a movingly evoked world, and a threatening background that licks flamelike along the edges of the scenario proper. Lois comes to life as neither Sydney nor Emmeline does; she is a human being with dimensions in excess of actual story requirements, and hence she escapes the sense of formulation that plagues her counterparts. A number of the people surrounding her likewise have this reverberative quality. Of Bowen's previous characters, perhaps only Markie Linkwater of *To the North* has a resonance equivalent to that possessed by *The Last September*'s Myra Naylor, Hugo Montmorency, and Marda Norton. Here, for the first time, the author employs contrasting settings effectively, which allows the depiction of the army huts to comment upon Danielstown and to evaluate it. This strategy foreshadows the successful use of similar pairings in novels to follow.

The Hotel

Although Sydney Warren is twenty-two when she comes to spend the winter at the northern Italian resort of *The Hotel* as the guest of an older, doting cousin, she is socially untried and is inexperienced with men. Though little is told of her past, we learn that she has been living a no-nonsense, academic life in London and has been seriously considering the study of medicine. By the time the book opens, Sydney has been identified by the hotel's other English guests as an aloof, rather cold, if attractive, person. She has established relationships with only one other individual, Mrs. Kerr, a middle-aged widow. This acquaintance is understandable since Mrs. Kerr is the most polished and knowledgeable of the guests in an assemblage composed chiefly of knitting and bridge-playing matrons. There are the three young Lawrence sisters, but they are vulgarly normal in their concerns with dancing and boys. Mrs. Kerr, who, like Sydney, holds herself above and apart from the others, has taken Sydney in hand as her protégée, and, naturally enough, she flatters her.

Two males enter this world. First comes an unmarried Anglican minister, James Milton, forty, and later, Mrs. Kerr's son Ronald, twenty-two. Midway through the novel, James proposes to Sydney; after first being refused, he is accepted. In the closing portion of the book, Sydney breaks the engagement, and the novel ends with James and Ronald, accidentally and ironically, departing together. The other characters, with the season drawing to a close, are preparing for the return to England.

Thus we are most immediately engaged in determining why James comes to propose, why Sydney accepts him and then breaks the engagement and why Sydney and Ronald do not become friends as by rights they seemingly should. Excepting the first of these questions, all of these queries bear upon the relationship between Mrs. Kerr and Sydney, as viewed by the latter. What the reader finally needs to comprehend is the implication of Sydney's angered final remarks to the older woman: "If there's one thing one might hope to learn from you it would be to be sickened and turned cold by cruelty and unfairness. . . . I am very grateful to you; you have done a great deal for me."[1]

It takes Sydney most of the novel and a considerable measure of anguish and distress to comprehend Mrs. Kerr's true nature. One of the novel's finest touches is its subtle opening scene, for a careful reading of it reveals Mrs. Kerr's self-interest from the start and adds sharpness to Sydney's blindness and gradual awakening. The book opens upon an agitated Miss Pym emerging from an argument with her companion, Miss Fitzgerald. Miss Pym, sick at heart, seeks to bring herself under control when confronted by the imposing Mrs. Kerr and is invited to walk with her toward the tennis courts. Mrs. Kerr sees at once that Miss Pym is upset, but she refuses to be involved in any way: "There were so many things that she might have said just now that Miss Pym could have taken up easily, but she did not say one of them, only exposed with indifference her profile to the sidelong, zealous search of Miss Pym" (15). Mrs. Kerr, aware that Sydney is awaiting her, hurries on oblivious of Miss Pym when they part: "Miss Pym spoke again, louder, but Mrs. Kerr, who was passing through the turnstile, gave no sign of attention" (19). For the present, Mrs. Kerr's elegant, exterior polish hides from Sydney her disciplined feelings, her ability to "[take] fashion in and subdue it and remain herself" (15).

A selfish person, Mrs. Kerr wishes to maintain control over her beautifully performed life, and this desire rules out the possibility of any involvement on the unstable and messy emotional level. Always cordially pleasant, she seeks to see and, so far as it is possible, to place everything in a pleasant light. But, even as a novice novelist, Bowen reveals artistic niceness by refraining from offering Mrs. Kerr as a one-dimensional dehumanized being with a stillborn heart. As a beautiful person, Mrs. Kerr has suffered from problems that confront life's golden children, or at least sometimes appear in their own eyes to confront them. She tells her son: "You see . . . I, who am what is called 'an attractive person,' am going to be lonelier than other people. . . ." When he reminds her that "A large number of people seemed to have loved" her, she replies, "No, no one, I think . . ." (256–57). Because she could be loved readily, she believes she could not be loved well. Her repression of her emotional life began, it may be assumed, simply as self-protection. The word with which she replaces "love" in her vocabulary and which she employs repeatedly is "fond."

Mrs. Kerr's response to Sydney's anger at the end of the novel cuts two ways. Her "Well, Sydney—what have I done?" is at once a measure of her emotional bankruptcy and a genuine response of surprise to conduct that has been, in her estimate, quite proper. It seems doubtful, finally, that she is sufficiently shaken by the rebuke to embark upon any self-renovation. But the closing encounter is overheard by Ronald, and evidently its substance, prepared for by earlier remarks by Sydney, touches him. He too appears to be "saved" from emotional disenfranchisement.

The early tennis court scene literally depicts the novel in miniature if the game is equated with life. Mrs. Kerr, who does not play, likes to sit by prettily and watch. Sydney, who has the reputation of being a good player (just as she has a reputation for brilliance), teams up with an older man, but, self-consciously aware that she is being watched by Mrs. Kerr, her game falls apart, and she and her partner are defeated. He feels let down, and Sydney becomes sharp with Mrs. Kerr. Sydney, indifferent to other people, acts almost as the lover of the fastidious older woman. She suffers until they are together; she is oversensitive in her presence; and she even thinks that, if she does not exist for her mentor as a player or person, she does not exist. It is only necessary to see Sydney with her good-hearted, simple, self-indulgent cousin Tessa (who is almost a parody of Mrs. Kerr) to register the impact that Mrs. Kerr has upon her. Sydney is at least in harmony with the other guests in holding Mrs. Kerr in awe.

Sydney herself is shortly being held in awe by James Milton. James, who goes to a walking picnic organized by Mr. and Mrs. Lee-Mittison without wearing his clerical collar, is flattered first by Sydney's company and then by being included, most gratifyingly, with the younger rather than with the older group of excursionists. Hitherto a confirmed bachelor, James, suddenly caught up in the spontaneity of the younger set, begins to suspect he may have been missing something in life. In his eyes, too, Sydney's poise and apparent maturity make her more desirable and accessible than does the frivolity of her peers. He slowly becomes enamored of her, and proposal is on the edge of his mind whether he recognizes it or not.

Meanwhile, Mrs. Kerr, who has reported the imminent arrival of Ronald, expresses the wish that Sydney and he will become good friends. This friendship is never realized, though both Sydney and he come to sense that, under different circumstances, they could have been friends and possibly more. Ronald proves reticent, touchy, and a shade arrogant, and, because of their respective unsettled natures, the events, and the inhibiting near command that they be friends, neither is able to act naturally.

Sydney intuitively gains her first fragile glimmering of Mrs. Kerr when the latter receives a letter from her "little boy." As Mrs. Kerr talks of her son, Sydney detects unnaturalness: "she felt herself beaten back by something that in spite of nature's whole precedent she knew for a falsity; an imposture her immaturity sensed but could not challenge" (99). With Ronald's arrival, Mrs. Kerr plays the part of devoted mother to the hilt; and this role involves the withdrawing of all attention from Sydney, a fortuitous possibility from Mrs. Kerr's viewpoint because of Sydney's increasing pressure on her dormant feelings. Thrown abruptly back upon herself and virtually jilted, Sydney suffers private hurt and public humiliation. It is into this situation James moves.

While he and Sydney are strolling in the neighboring hills, he, as he had no intention of doing, suddenly proposes. Both of them are genuinely startled, but Sydney's automatic response is to refuse him. But by the time they are together again, Sydney has experienced a series of events that cause her to reverse her decision. First, she and a child, Cordelia Barry, have walked past an Italian cemetery and "In such a mood she was not proof against the ordinary reflections on morality as she looked with Cordelia through the cemetery gates" (134). It is, however, less death than "the treachery of a future that must give one to death finally that oppresses her" (135). She is suddenly impressed by James who, she assumes, must have seen her as "ice-bound"; and she sees that his proposal "appeared in the light of present considerations heroic . . ." (136).

Second, Sydney has been confronted by the most dashing of the Lawrence girls, Veronica, who tells Sydney of her own engagement to Victor Ammering, but leads up to it circuitously. Unknowingly, Sydney questions the merit of the bland young man, and Veronica, an extroverted modern young woman, seeks to justify her relations with Victor who has not been popular with the hotel adults. Veronica reveals that Sydney has no copyright on disenchantment, for she tells Sydney: "You see, I've got absolutely no illusions. I do feel I might have been terribly fond of somebody. . . ." She asks Sydney if she "thinks perhaps men aren't what they used to be?" And in a final disclosure adds, "I must marry somebody. You see, I must have some children" (158). Veronica's willingness to compromise her possibilities for fulfillment is rather heady stuff. Sydney is left confronting the vapory nature of happiness: if not for Veronica, for whom then?

Sydney's third and final preparation for engagement occurs in a conversation with Mrs. Kerr as they sit in a *patisserie*. After discussing Ronald, they turn to Sydney's "bitterness" over her treatment at the hands of Mrs. Kerr, who comments: "I begin now to guess you've expected much more of me, and that I've been taking and taking without so much as a glance ahead or a single suspicion of what you would want back." Sydney, chilled by this cool analysis, can "only suppose that cruelty as supremely disinterested as art had, like art, its own purity, which could transcend anything and consecrate the nearest material to its uses" (181–82). In the light of these revelations, the engagement becomes both reasonable and desirable. And it might be added that the book Sydney is reading offstage is Thomas Hardy's *Jude the Obscure*.

Sydney's acceptance is an act of cowardice and movement from rather than toward life. She projects the safe, uneventful existence that marriage with James ensures. To her married life seems preferable to the ambushes to which her formless life and vague future seem certain to expose her. One of the first to suspect the true nature of the ensuing engagement is, of course, the incisive Mrs. Kerr. In a graciously veiled conversation with James, she causes him to suffer, yet the ambiguous nature of her being leaves the reader wondering whether she is unfeelingly cruel or calculatingly wise. When she says, "her loving you . . . her loving you absolutely . . . ," James grimaces, for Sydney has just admitted to him not only her lack of love but her hope of finding some for him (211). If James, nevertheless, cannot bring himself to break off the affair, he is at least sympathetic with Sydney's feelings when she later announces that she will not marry him.

Sydney must, of course, see into the truth of the situation for herself. The path to this recognition also follows a three-step preparation: conversations with first Ronald and then James, followed by a motor-car ride along a narrow, twisting road cut into steep cliffs. While out walking, Ronald comes upon Sydney sitting on a rock awaiting James. While they chat, Sydney suddenly becomes aware of the naïveté running beneath Ronald's apparent sophistication, but, more importantly, she recognizes in his views a portrait of herself: "While Ronald talked she often had a giddy sense of watching all she had ever said being wound off from a spool again backwards" (222). When Ronald rises to go, Sydney feels a rush of "panic" and begs him not to leave her alone. Thus, when James arrives, Sydney's emergent uncertainty and her apparent determination to harden herself for her fate causes him more pain. As James listens to her berate happiness, "he could have wept for her . . ." (235). Sydney's final awakening comes in an epiphany born of shock in a scene that nicely balances the earlier one in the Italian cemetery. While being driven down the steep cliffside road, Sydney envisions the car plunging over the precipice carrying herself, James, Tessa, and Mrs. Kerr to death. When the car has to stop suddenly because the narrow road is blocked, she instantly sees she must go on living. The sense of life's fleetingness that she had experienced in the cemetery is replaced by an insight into its preciousness: "she for the first time felt life sharply, life as keen as death to bite upon the consciousness . . ." (245).

When telling James of her decision, she explains: "I suppose it was the shock of being alive. . . . I had no idea we were as real as this. I'd never realized it mattered so much . . ." (247). It may be seen that Sydney, as well as other of Bowen heroines, has affinities with Sleeping Beauty.

Some critical tears have been shed for James, but these result from a failure to consider his basically robust nature and from the fact that the whole experience opens new vistas of life hitherto unavailable to him. He is quite aware of the truth of Sydney's act: "At this moment of the swing apart he was one with her, and was able to say, she is right" (249). Other marriages in the book represent a fate that James and Sydney have most probably averted. The speculative reader might well suspect that James and Sydney would have been similar to Colonel and Mrs. Duperriere of *The Last September.*

Sydney's act is an affirmation of honest feeling and also a refusal to give up on the vital possibilities of life. Her final anger with Mrs. Kerr, whom she sees as largely responsible for her near entombment, is cleansing, and in turn, it is perhaps restorative for others. In being true both to the society depicted in the novel and to her reading of life, the author quite properly leaves Sydney's future tentative. It is evident Sydney is now ready to begin the true, the awakened, ascent of life. As for the village at the summit, however, it "may be deserted." Like Lawrence's *The Rainbow*, *The Hotel* tells of a girl who has survived a rigorous preparation for adulthood; both novels end by promising no more than promise.

The Last September

The Last September tells of the last month that Lois Farquar, a nineteen-year-old orphan, spends with her aunt and uncle at Danielstown, one of Ireland's big country houses. It is 1920, the time of the Irish Troubles, of rebels and Blacks and Tans; the sounds of lorries and reports of battle provide the matrix of the action. Lois is another of Bowen's innocents who passes through the twilight zone separating adolescence from adulthood. Introspective and self-conscious, Lois does not know what to do with herself, but she is most anxious to do something. She asks an older woman, "Did you have any difficulty about beginning?"[2] In the preface of the novel's reissue in 1951, Bowen reveals the autobiographical nature of this question by recalling that she asked herself during youthful summers spent at Bowen's Court, "*what* I should be, and when?" (*Afterthought*, 96). The novel arrives at an ironic conclusion: Lois's desire for something to happen fulfills itself though in ways unexpected.

From the start, Lois's situation does not appear promising, positioned as she is between the moribund Protestant landlord tradition, represented by Sir Richard and Lady Myra Naylor, and the progressively threatening political upheaval. Yet time provides everything necessary for her subsequent two-stage fall from innocence. Fortunately, the sense of contrivance that marks *The Hotel* is absent. Bowen is very much at home in this work "which of all my books," she writes in *Afterthought*, "is nearest my heart" (96). The story has a strong sense of dramatic inevitability and unrolls in the vividly evoked world of Danielstown, which is a powerful presence throughout.

Since the story seeks to pinpoint the time when Lois begins to have a life of her own, it is set clearly in the past—the only Bowen novel employing this perspective. This sense of completion is necessary since only in retrospect can we possibly presume to identify turning points or locate significance where, at the time, none was recognizable. Appropriately, the book creates and sustains a sense of unreality that conveys Lois's vague and unresolved perception of experience.

Initially, the run of tennis parties and house guests elicit little more than superficial interest from Lois. Her ostensible beau is one of the locally stationed young English army officers, Gerald Lesworth, who is sincere and gentlemanly but too much the obliging mannequin. Though warmly welcomed at Danielstown, Gerald does not stand high in the estimate of Myra because of his modest background. Lois, wanting to love him, wishes he were more unpredictable and disconcerting; but these qualities he never manages to possess.

Chief among the earlier houseguests are Hugo Montmorency and his wife, long-standing Naylor friends. Hugo, once the boyfriend of Lois's mother, is an unhappy individual. A wanderer who makes his home from one visit to the next, he is, in Hemingway's phrase, an arrested adolescent. An introspective dreamer, he has periodically projected big plans for himself, but he has never had the capacity to realize them. Consequently, he is a tense man, and he is touchy because, in his estimate, his position belies his abilities. Thematically, he stands as a warning of what retained innocence can become. His impotence, however, is far from unique since it really reflects the general dependence and futility of the Anglo-Irish.

Narratively, Hugo is involved in the first stage of Lois's preparation for maturity. He develops a crush on another Danielstown visitor, Marda Norton, who arrives from England on the verge of thirty and a rich London marriage. An attractive creature of sophistication and aloofness, she impresses Lois and prompts her to personal confidences: "Being grown up seems trivial, somehow. I mean, dressing and writing notes instead of letters, and trying to make impressions. When you have to think so much of what other people feel about you there seems no time to think what you feel about them" (136). When she submits her amateurish artwork to Marda for comment, Marda tells her it is not good. When Lois retells her egocentric dreams to Marda, Marda tells her: "But be interested in what happens to you for its own sake; don't expect to be touched or changed—or to be in anything that you do" (139). For herself, Marda knows her wisdom, "fruit of her own relations to experience," has been acquired at the price of exhaustion. She regards marriage as a haven that will save her from the wear and tear of existence. But she does remain a capable young woman; quite conscious of her impact upon Hugo, she does not doubt her capacity to handle him.

Lois, Marda, Hugo, and the key themes of violence and awareness merge in a major scene near the close of the second of the novel's three books. The scene witnesses Lois's entrance into a new plane of comprehension. Walking together through a woods, the threesome come upon an old, abandoned mill. Hugo, angered by Marda's playful teasing, settles down on a rock for a smoke and a sulk while the two women push on to inspect the crumbling building. Inside, they come upon and surprise an Irish rebel who has been resting; he points a pistol at them but when they swear silence on the encounter he begins to withdraw. Weak from hunger, however, he slips, the gun goes off accidentally, and the back of Marda's hand is grazed. Hugo, who comes running full-tilt, shouts out Marda's name, and a note in his voice strikes Lois more forcefully than has the confrontation with the rebel. Even Hugo, preoccupied with Marda's wound, looks at Lois and has "distantly, some apprehension of an emotional shock" (175). Hugo wishes to dash into the mill but is blocked by Lois and Marda, true to their pledge to allow the rebel to withdraw. Once again angered and feeling exposed, Hugo stalks off. Alone, the women briefly retreat into silence in order to adjust themselves, before Lois says, "I've had a . . . revelation. . . . I was too damned innocent" (177). The revelation of Hugo's love of which she had been oblivious better serves to acquaint Lois with life in the present. Lois, naturally allowing her mind to drift into the future, suddenly tells Marda, "It's harder, for some reason, to imagine what I'll be doing or where I shall be" (178).

Appropriately, as the novel's third part opens, Lois, with her new sense of alertness, is positioned for the first time outside her own Danielstown environs. The occasion is a party in one of the huts provided for married army officers and their wives in the nearby village. The raucous, sensual, chaotic scene presents a nice contrast to the Naylor world. The brash affair is easily accessible to Lois as reality, and here she decides she and Gerald are in love. Not certain where events are leading, Lois thinks, "All the same . . . it is something definite" (223). Myra Naylor recognizes quickly enough that Lois's love is superficial and she tells her, "Real feeling explains itself . . . ," and proposes that with autumn approaching Lois go off to art college (231).

Myra then arranges an assignation with Gerald, and her handling of him is dazzling if unfair, for he is no match for her forensic abilities. His inexperience and immaturity are humorously exposed. And, when he draws up his last thrust, "You're not going to stop my seeing her," she replies: "I don't know what sort of girls' mothers and aunts you're accustomed to . . . but how could you expect me to do such a preposterous thing? . . . You know we are always delighted to see you at any time" (250–51). In a state of bewilderment, Gerald himself volunteers as they part, "I promise I won't kiss her" (251).

Myra is one of the finest touches in the book, for Bowen does not allow her to become the stock figure her role in the story implies. A staunch defender of the Danielstown tradition, she suffers from a social narrowness verging on the snobbish; but she is no figure of fun. A robust defender of civilization, she is prepared to act when her high values are threatened. When her home falls at the close, she stands forth stoically as a figure not to be defeated by life.

Gerald meets Lois in the woods of Danielstown for the "frank talk" Marda has urged him to have with her. Lois—already apprised of what has taken place through Francie Montmorency who, ironically has acted "courageously" for the first time in her life in a cause with feet of clay—is more chagrined than hurt that Gerald has meekly accepted Marda's insistence that Lois does not really love him. Her badgering does not convince him: "She watched with agony what seemed to be his indifference" (261). As they part, she may have tears in her eyes, but she maintains sufficient presence of mind to take comfort in the fact that, with summer drawing to a close, the necessity for tennis parties has ended. Earlier, the narrative voice reported that "Lois looked and strained after feeling, but felt nothing. Her problem was, not only *how* to get out unseen, but *why*, to what purpose?" (183). Lois had seen Gerald as her "how," but she had overlooked an answer to the "why." The feelings that have propelled her relationship with Gerald have been contrived. When she experiences genuine emotion, her ersatz feelings are exposed. Lois, like Sydney before her, comes alive in confronting the reality of death: "Life, seen whole for a moment, was one act of apprehension, the apprehension of death" (277).

Before her impending departure for college, Lois is given a test that permits her to show that she is both able to act upon true feelings, even when she does not feel socially confident, and to defend the standards of her tradition. Unannounced, two silly army wives drive into Danielstown, "shrieking and waving" because they really wish to have a look into the privacy of an aristocratic drawing room. When Lois confronts them she is courteous, nervous, and resolute: "she seemed determined to keep them out" (270). Never having entered the house, the wives leave.

The novel moves swiftly to its close. When word arrives that Gerald has been killed in an ambush while on patrol, Lois accepts the news quietly. Once she had told Marda she would like to act tragically; now she has her opportunity. Instead she is very conscious of what the Danielstown people will feel for her and what she will owe them: "She saw that for days ahead she must not deny humanity, she would have no privacy" (276–77). This death, which carries no tragic overtones as the title of the novel's last part, "The Departure of Gerald," suggests, is taken as the occasion for Lois's own departure into new realms of experience. The reader is simply informed that she has gone to France to perfect her French. That she has not gone to study art may indicate a growth in her capacity for self-judgment—her personal recognition of a lack of talent.

The novel closes with the burning of Danielstown—an episode that completes the simple but profound implication that life consists of loss and gain. In her preface to the novel Bowen asks, "Was it sorrow to Lois, Danielstown's burning?" (*Afterthought*, 99). The proper answer is surely, "yes, and no." For Marda had once observed that "What Hugo needs is real trouble" (159). The deepest of Lois's feelings belonged to Danielstown; in its loss we are perhaps to read a critical touch to her education. Told with wit, *The Last September* conveys mellowness and a sense of life's shadowed underside. Hermoine Lee rightly sees that for the first time Bowen maintains "a successful relationship between a comedy of manners and the underlying pull of fatality."[3]

To the North

Elizabeth Bowen's most dramatic rendering of the dangers of preserved innocence is in *To the North*. In no other novel is she so close to the world of fairy tale as the names of several characters suggest. The imagery identifying the heroine, Emmeline Summers, and her lover, Markie Linkwater, reveals the radical nature of the work; she is likened repeatedly to an angel; he is characterized as satanic and malevolent. She is an "orphan of a dislocated century"; he, a "natural offspring" of it. The novel has been likened to Jacobean tragedy because of its combination of a brooding sense of foreboding and comic byplay.

Critics have regarded the book as a testament to the impossibility for true love in our era. True enough, the novel displays little that is normative; feelings are depicted as either anemic or corrupt, but a less sentimental consideration reveals Bowen as not writing against the age so much as using it to update her age-old problem. She daringly juxtaposes the most idealistic of all her innocents and the most "wastelandish" of all her landscapes, and her point surely is that innocence has never been such a potential liability. Emmeline's apparently deliberate killing of Markie and herself is as much a comment on her own inhumanity as on the conditions of her environment, perhaps even more so.

Theoretically, Emmeline has the formula for a rich existence. Publicly, she is willingly in tune with the business of the world—with affairs presented largely through her concern with travel, rail, air, and motor. Emmeline and her partner run their travel agency chiefly on élan, and she loves driving her car. But she chooses to keep her private and subjective lives quite apart from this active public one. The private is to be ordered and mannerly, but the subjective is to be vitally emotional. Though twenty-five, she does not doubt the possibility of an ideal love affair. Emmeline has instinctively an awareness and respect for feeling that Lois Farquar had to discover, but she has not learned as did Lois, the necessity for sharp vision. This fact is pointedly established by her myopia, requiring her to wear glasses. However, her pride keeps her from donning them on social occasions, so that she moves both literally and figuratively through a half-world of shadows. Appropriately enough, Markie does not like to see her wearing glasses.

The author develops various ironic situations based on Emmeline's sight. For example, Julian Tower, the man to whom her sister-in-law Cecilia eventually becomes engaged, has an affinity for Emmeline that she cannot comprehend and that he, because of diffidence, does not press. But the reader is aware he is the very man, as his surname implies, who in his kindness and responsibility would provide her a haven and educate her.

Markie registers with Emmeline because he is different, informal, and humorous compared to the reserved men she knows. He has an emotional current to which she responds, though she is incapable of seeing its superficial, even twisted, nature. Her lack of perception follows the author's having already established how readily Cecilia sized him up on their first encounter. For Markie, feelings are a source of excitement. They are also threatening because, as a son of the century, he suffers from Eliot's "dissociation of sensibility": his feelings are apart from and not subject to the control of the rational mind—"The edge of his mind was restless with superstition: like natives before the solid advance of imperial forces, aspiration, feeling, all sense of the immaterial had retreated in him before reason to some craggy hinterland where, having made no terms with the conqueror, they were submitted to no control and remained a menace. Like savages coming to town on a fair day to skip and chaffer, travestying their character in strange antics, creating by their very presence a saturnalia in which the conqueror may unbend, feeling crept out in him from some unmapped region" (204). An interesting touch is Markie's inability to drive and his dislike of cars; as a sensualist, he naturally abhors what is cold and mechanical. Cecilia claims he has "a Byron complex," and he is characterized as "a voluptuary" (201).

The first half of the novel might be entitled "Emmeline Triumphant": home life on Oudenarde Road with Cecilia is pleasant and secure; her affair with Markie is increasingly more satisfying; and the new travel-agency business, with its motto "Travel Dangerously," is a success. Cecilia's Aunt Georgina, fluttering about like a brood hen, is dubious about Emmeline's involvement with Markie but she cannot be taken seriously by either Cecilia or Emmeline since she is forever manufacturing issues: she is "quick to detect situations that [do] not exist" and is prepared to enlarge "her own life in ripples of apprehension on everybody's behalf" (22). Naturally enough this "wolf, wolf," situation contributes to Emmeline's downfall. Cecilia is also rendered more ineffectual in Emmeline's cause by her idée fixe that a girl with Emmeline's nature could never love a man like Markie who is such a poseur. Additionally disarming for her intimates is Emmeline's fastidious concern for privacy; for, incapable of distrusting the intentions of others, she cannot conceive of anyone's committing indiscretions against her subjective sense of reality. This penchant for circumspection goes unchallenged because she enjoys the reputation of a sensible girl with a good head for business. In any event, Cecilia notes that the orphaned Emmeline "has done what she likes" since she was twelve (223).

So far as Emmeline is concerned, the climax of her life occurs when her public and private lives momentarily coincide. With business flourishing, she and her partner decide to arrange a tie-in with two young men in Paris who also have a small but prospering travel agency. When Emmeline agrees to fly to them for talks, Markie decides he will accompany her for the weekend. In Paris, they sleep together, and, for a brief span, life peaks gloriously. Bowen records this romantic interlude in the most idyllic passages in her fiction. This flight records, however, the height from which Emmeline must crash. The remainder of the novel traces her downward curve.

Actually a crack appears before the trip, an incident both forewarning of the future and signaling—or, ironically, failing to signal—the dangers of the unobserved life to Emmeline. She is ambushed when she is alone in the office with the secretary, suitably named Miss Tripp. Coming upon Emmeline, Miss Tripp accuses her of heartlessness, implies a considerable fondness for her, and volunteers that she has been dressing for Emmeline. Emmeline is stunned because of her own ignorance of what should have been obvious enough. At the same time, this unsuspected human capacity for perversity comes to her as a revelation. (There is reason to believe her partner, Peter Lewis, is homosexual, something else of which Emmeline is ignorant.) Upset for the afternoon, Emmeline does not transfer to her private life the lesson provided by Miss Tripp. When Miss Tripp is soon replaced by Miss Armitage, the informal and exciting days at the office are numbered. Wonderfully efficient, Miss Armitage progressively takes over until the partners are little more than accessories. Furthermore, Emmeline's private life becomes more troubled, and the travel agency is further dispirited by bad weather and European political tensions.

In the background, Cecilia and Julian have been seeing each other regularly, and Cecilia, though she first hesitates, finally agrees to wed him. Word of the engagement, of what in effect means the impending end of the secure life at Oudenarde Road, reaches Emmeline by telegram at a most inappropriate moment. Hoping to restage the exhilarating Paris weekend with Markie, she borrows a remote sylvan cottage from an acquaintance for a weekend. Envisioning Edenic hours with her love, Emmeline makes elaborate preparations to wine and dine him sumptuously. Therefore, she becomes conscious of a change in the atmosphere when, just after they have completed a lengthy drive, Markie insists they backtrack to a village for a meal that Emmeline had proposed to prepare. The romantic cottage, complete with a golden harp, provides an ironic setting for this disclosure of an ailing affair in which she has invested so much of herself. At this point she learns of Cecilia's decision, and the weekend is aborted.

Markie returns from the lost weekend to seek out his old, easy-going girlfriend Daisy, an act he has been gradually fomenting. The strain of Emmeline has become too much for him; he has been frightened of her pure, intense, and demanding love, her "exhausting exultation." He feels emotionally incapable of sustaining Emmeline's golden concept of their relationship. Eventually, her ability to bear his absence crumples, and she calls him. When his telephone is answered by Daisy, Emmeline is chilled and becomes somnambulistic.

With Hardyesque irony, Cecilia and Julian, at Georgina's insistence, now invite Markie to dinner, for they are unaware of the rift between him and Emmeline. Markie appears and "the incalculable [flares] out"—he finds himself "ambushed," for the "unforeseen beauty" of Emmeline prompts "the violent resurgence of his desire" (312). As Emmeline, at the conclusion of the evening, drives him from London to his destination "to the north," he not only urges her to return with him to his flat, he also urges a return to their former relationship; he even proposes marriage. But Emmeline knows there is no going back: once lost, always lost for paradise. To his importuning she replies: "And tell the same story again and again and again? There's nothing more left ahead of us" (319). All she now desires is "quiet."

Baffled by her, Markie stares discontentedly at the dashboard, "at the two lit dials: the clock, the speedometer" (322). Driving furiously, Emmeline seems determined to eclipse both time and space, to move swiftly through the remainder of her life. Markie senses "her speed [has] the startled wildness of flight . . . she [is] like someone who plays the piano wildly to drown some crisis they cannot even admit . . ." (324). She drives "as though away from the ashy destruction of everything" (325).

At the end, Emmeline blames only herself for what has happened and she feels no anger against Markie or the times: "'One does oneself in,' she said" (322). In one sense, she is right; her own sense of purity has prevented her from meeting the world on factual terms. But her self-accusation is really the ironic defense of the self-oriented position she has manned throughout. The interconnectedness of life has not registered with her; otherness is beyond her, which is the point of the inset story of the sailor who is moved to kiss her cheek, as well as that of the Miss Tripp interlude. Emmeline is at last to be identified as an narcissist. The repeated emphasis upon her beauty, her passivity, and her eyesight provides the clues to her trouble. Nothing has disturbed her peace; her beauty has been both protective cocoon and sufficient reason for gentle treatment by the passing world. Miss Bowen tells nothing of

Emmeline's past because there is nothing to record; she has not had the gradual training that prepares individuals for life's rude and inevitable shocks. Markie, on the other hand—and this is one of the book's master touches of irony—does progress to awareness and to a greater sense of responsibility toward others. He is capable at the last of self-judgment, of "self-contempt, and a maddening resentment of his desire . . ." (312). Markie, whatever distortions he has harbored, can be seen to have always had the heat of life within. Increasingly terrified by her speed and trancelike driving, Markie speaks her name "hopelessly," and, "as though hearing her name on his lips for the first time, dazzled, she turned to smile" (327). She, it appears, has already found herself in the promised land and she is joyous to discover Markie's presence. In the instant of distraction, the car plunges head-on into another, killing everyone involved. The rendering of this last ride together is one of the finest passages in all of Bowen's work.

To the North carries the subsidiary story of Pauline, age fourteen, Julian's ward. Pauline, like Emmeline, an orphan, is not astigmatic. Her growing awareness of the adult world provides a humorous balance to the main plot, as well as a means of placing it. Also like Emmeline, Pauline comes as a visitor to Georgina's country home, Faraways, but Pauline's experiences there are quite different. Surrounded by the human oddities that Georgina has a passion for collecting, Pauline develops her powers of alertness rapidly. She concludes from her experience that "she [will] never feel safe again" (214). Rabbitlike, Pauline is learning she must make her own way in the world, and, conscious of other people surrounding her, she is "anxious to please . . ." (219). She is also capable of sharing a confidence with Cecilia. Pauline, to employ the imagery of the novel, is traveling on a different "line" from that of Emmeline. But Emmeline, in driving "to the north," becomes, in the Lawrencean imagery of *Women in Love*, fulfilled in the frozen reaches of self-love.

Chapter Three
The Disruptive Children

> Especially the crimes that spring from love seem right and fair from the actor's point of view. . . .
> —R. W. Emerson, "Experience"

After leaving her first two heroines, Sydney and Lois, in a vague limbo following their escapes from false love affairs, it is hardly surprising that Elizabeth Bowen in subsequent novels explores later stages of a woman's career. And, with her penchant for young women who entangle themselves with the wrong man, no other variation on her previous stories could be more dramatic than not to have her heroine escape—what occurs to Emmeline in *To the North*. In the three novels of the second group—*Friends and Relations* (1931), *The House in Paris* (1935), and *The Death of the Heart* (1938)—Bowen continues to explore various consequences stemming from apparently disastrous (in the eyes of the protagonists) early romances. Each book is structured on a pattern of "before" and "after"—before the disappointment of love and following it. The emphasis in two of the books—*Friends and Relations* and *The Death of the Heart*—falls upon the aftermath in which the heroine, years after being hurt, comes to terms with her damaged feelings and painful memories: in so doing, she gains for herself a more promising relationship with her husband. The third novel, *The House in Paris*, centers upon the melodramatic early story; it traces step-by-step the young woman's unlikely and painful self-betrayal.

The author's recognition of the potential impact on life of violence or unexpected intrusion continues to manifest itself, but with a new variation. Her earlier motifs of accident, warfare, and speed are now given human embodiment, for each novel includes a child, or childlike persons with demonic propensities. Ultimately, their disruptive acts rupture the apparently polished surface of life and permit buried feelings to rise and re-energize existence. The three books also witness an evolution of the artistic success of this character: in *Friends and Relations* she is poorly integrated into the narrative, and her eventual actions are distressingly arbitrary; in *The House in Paris* she is less contrived; but in *The Death of the Heart* she is a perfectly natural function of the story.

These three novels also represent a progression in another way. While the subject matter of these works is intrinsically richer than in the first trio, it presents technical difficulties that Bowen only partially resolves. For instance, the tight integration of *The Last September* is missing from both *Friends and Relations* and *The House in Paris*, which have ten-year gaps between the first part of the narrative and the subsequent one. Bowen handles the problem more successfully in *Friends and Relations* than in *The House in Paris*, but not until *The Death of the Heart* does she manage to regain the aesthetic integrity of *The Last September*. *The Death of the Heart* is the author's supreme artistic triumph: James Hall calls it "a monument, one of a kind."[1] In a very real sense, it is the consequence and culmination of the author's first five novels.

A third of the way into *Friends and Relations* the narrative jumps ahead ten years to the time when the feelings initiated in the opening sequence, which have had a subterranean existence in the intervening years, suddenly well up. This great leap forward produces an uncomfortable effect, and the resulting sense of contrivance is never overcome. In retrospect, it appears regrettable that the early material was not introduced into the present story as flashback. *The House in Paris* does begin with the present scene and does raise interest in the causes behind the effects being shown. The lengthy midsection reverts to the past, and then the third part of the novel returns to the present and resumes where the opening section left off. This approach gives the past a sense of drama entirely absent from the corresponding portion of *Friends and Relations*. Still, *The House in Paris* leaves an aftertaste of dissatisfaction because the obvious drama of the missing years is never adequately realized, and the reader's expectations are not fulfilled. The novel suffers additional difficulties that I later discuss.

The Death of the Heart is the kind of novel an author undoubtedly aims for each time he undertakes one. Every decision seems to be correct, and all of the disparate components are harmonized. The past, the present, and the intervening years are all realized at once in the first third of the novel. The remainder of the narrative is devoted not merely to the laying of a troublesome past but to the emerging issues of the present. Bowen's master stroke is in having two heroines. She combines the story that concerned her in the first group of novels, of first love, with her more recent narrative interest. The younger heroine becomes in this way a correlative for the earlier years of the older one. Actually, the central impact of the story derives less from the outcome of the first love or the confrontation with debilitating memories than from the dynamic relationship of the two women.

The Death of the Heart is an impressive novel in any case, but, when we view it in the context of the author's earlier work, its triumphs even more forcefully impress us. Like an iceberg, five-sixths of the novel bulks beneath the surface.

Friends and Relations

Friends and Relations opens with a marriage, and a second soon follows. Handsome Edward Tilney chooses as his bride Laurel Studdart, a gentle, attractive Cheltenham girl with a pleasant, low-keyed personality and a true love for her husband. Edward is also loved, and more passionately, by Janet Studdart, Laurel's sister. But not until later in the narrative is the reader apprised of Edward's awareness of his attraction to Janet. In the lengthy introductory wedding scene, the principals are seen only fleetingly: Edward and Laurel as a radiant couple; Janet as a hard-working organizer. As they appear to the assembled guests, so do they appear to the reader; there are only the barest hints of deeper emotional currents. These, however, register in the unusual mind of an unattractive girl of fifteen, Theodora Thirdman; indeed, much of the scene is observed from her eccentric point of view.

The daughter of ineffectual parents whom she bullies, Theodora feels bound to make some useful contacts for them since they have recently returned from living in Switzerland and are quite out of touch. Doomed to little success, Theodora does adversely attract the attention of the bridegroom's mother, Lady Elfrida, who calls her "A terrible girl" in response to which Theodora comments to herself, "We shall meet again."[2] And, indeed, they do. With a mind alerted to the deep and the hidden, Theodora grasps not only that Janet loves Edward but also that Lady Elfrida much prefers Janet to Laurel. Having ascribed a sense of despair to Janet, Theodora feels a strong attraction for her.

Two weeks after the wedding Janet visits friends and meets Rodney Meggatt of Batts Abbey. Four weeks later, when they announce their engagement, the immediate repercussions from a distressed Edward temporarily suspend it. Rodney's uncle, the explorer and big-game hunter Considine Meggatt, proves to have been Lady Elfrida's correspondent some years earlier. (It is eventually disclosed that Janet was fully aware of this background information when she became engaged.) Though a child at the time of the divorce proceedings, Edward has been scarred by the affair that saw his mother leave his father, who died shortly thereafter, even though she does not wed Considine. Edward's near neurotic touchiness over the whole matter is as expected additionally exacerbated when Janet arrives in London to holiday with Lady Elfrida, ostensibly to shop for her trousseau.

The first show of feelings between Janet and Edward occurs at Elfrida's apartment. He accuses her of not loving Rodney; she retorts that Edward is "like a malicious, horrible child" (72). Only years later in a soul-searching conversation with Elfrida does Janet confess the truth that she accepted Rodney impulsively in order to become really involved with the Tilney family. Janet can claim only inexperience for her youthful action: "I thought we might all feel better afterwards; I didn't know it would last. You see, you see, I had no experience, nothing outside myself" (151).

Two-thirds of the novel takes place, as I have indicated, ten years following the opening ceremony. The Tilneys now live in London, Edward works in a Whitehall office, and they have two children, Anna and Simon. The Meggatts, who live at Batts Abbey where Rodney conducts a large farming operation, have a daughter, Hermoine. The families periodically gather at the Abbey, but they do so only when Considine is absent, which is frequently. When the narrative resumes, Janet and Rodney are on the verge of a significant decision but do not recognize it as such. It is summer, and Anna and Simon are vacationing with them. Considine, who is at "loose ends," is also present, and Janet thinks it would be opportune if Elfrida were invited to visit as company for him. In deference to Edward's feelings, Janet and Rodney have never brought the former lovers together, but now, after all these years, there seems little reason not to do so if Elfrida will come, and she is quite prepared to do so.

Wishing to act quite openly, Janet writes to tell Edward and Laurel what has transpired and then braces for any reaction from London, but none comes. Now another visitor arrives—Theodora. Outwardly, she has grown into an attractive woman; inwardly, she remains the abrasive enfant terrible. She decides Batts Abbey is boring, Janet is languid, and the presence of Elfrida and Considine is fascinating. Having looked the situation over thoroughly, she concludes: "I daresay it's time *something* happened" (109). Unbeknownst to anyone, she sends off a letter to Laurel. Shortly thereafter, Edward, maintaining distress at the children's exposure to the corrupt couple, suddenly descends upon the Abbey to claim them. Since the exposure has been in progress for several days, Janet is taken aback. But, in a private discussion, Edward shows Janet Theodora's letter, and it is evident he has been upset by her hints of lovelessness between Janet and Rodney. When Janet says to him, "you need never have come," he replies, "I had to see you. . ." (136). This confrontation stirs their latent feelings for each other, and a showdown between them appears unavoidable. Edward, unsettled, leaves with his children, but a few days later a troubled Janet boards a train for London; she is intent upon talking to Laurel and resolving her own uneasiness.

The events that transpire suggest that the title of the novel's third section, "The Fine Week," contains a pun. The weather is lovely, but events call for delicate handling, and, for a time, Janet and Edward tread very fragile ground. Prior to the trip and while en route, Janet undergoes the Jamesian experience of sensing the presence of a phantomlike alternative being: "a grotesque, not quite impossible figure, had come to interpose between herself and Laurel. A woman, an unborn shameful sister, travestying their two natures, enemy to them both" (173). Janet hopes, in seeing Laurel, to excise this figure. When she does not find Laurel at home, Janet joins Edward for lunch. Inescapably, they meet now "as lovers" (170). Before the day is over, Janet has her talk with Laurel, has Edward to her hotel room, and in the small hours of the morning she returns to the Abbey where she is not expected. Adultery has not been committed, though Edward has tempted it saying, "can't we comfort each other?" (190). Janet, however, refuses.

Evidently, Edward has been attracted to Janet from the first, but, recognizing her potentially passionate nature, he was afraid of her—afraid to trust her to the future and afraid too of his own feelings. With Janet and Elfrida on his own doorstep, his skittishness has been understandable. The novel implies a distinction between love and passion, or the romantic will. Both Janet and Edward are well loved by their mates, and, even though neither marriage is in any way passionate, this absence of deep feeling in no way justifies marital destruction. Janet's explanation to Edward for her position is brief and to the point: "we have no—no bitter necessity" (190). Almost defying the sentimental reader to view her conclusion as simply the triumph of the family over personal desire, Bowen has Janet play hostess the next day to the Mother's Union.

Edward leaves Janet feeling a great sense of release: "He supposed he must now be delivered from something, free: this term with no bounds, incapable of appreciation, of measurement, spun in his head . . ." (210). He is welcomed home by Laurel who has just reexamined and reassessed her love for him and found it authentic. Simultaneously, Janet and Rodney, who is innocent of what has transpired, talk, and, though she makes the remark in reference to furniture, Janet's comment that "we must reorganize" says what is necessary.

Faded away again into the background is Theodora, the nemesis, the saving dark goddess who had acted because she felt Edward held a "mortmain on Janet's spirit" (112). The attitude of the Meggatts to her is "fatalistic."

Perhaps it is significant that this strange forceful woman shares a flat with a creative writer. But as interesting as Theodora is as a character, she is one of the several unsatisfactory aspects of the book. While she conveys the author's sense of the unexpectedness of life and the saving possibilities inherent in it, she functions too neatly as a deus ex machina. Elsewhere Bowen is more successful in having her source of shock spring from her foreground material. Another weak link is the characterization of Edward, for, since we see him almost perpetually ill-tempered, like a miffed child in the midst of adults, it is hard to accept as real the feelings lavished upon him by both Janet and Laurel. And, too, the sensitivity he bears toward his mother's past is unconvincing.

Furthermore, Bowen spends too much time on material that is too peripheral to the central drama. The long wedding scene, Laurel's luncheon party, the visit of the Tilney children to the Abbey ultimately are all so much filler. Perhaps the author's decision to tell the story from the beginning instead of commencing with the present scene and slowly disclosing the past was unfortunate. *Friends and Relations* anticipates Miss Bowen's later novels, *A World of Love* and *The Little Girls*, in its concern with buried emotional potential; in each of these later novels, the gradual and fragmented insertion of exposition is employed to intensify the rising drama. No other Bowen novel is so strategically weak as *Friends and Relations*.

The House in Paris

The core of *The House in Paris* is the episode in which Karen Michaelis, twenty-three, the engaged daughter of a refined upper-middle-class London family, meets the fiancé of her best friend in Hythe and goes to bed with him. Half of the novel investigates how this affair happened; the other half, divided into two parts as a frame, takes place in the present, ten years later, and records the absorption or normalizing of the earlier event.

The poles of the story are two houses, the Michaelis home in London and Mme Fisher's house in Paris. Karen proves a rebel to the staid, stable home of her parents; Naomi, Karen's best friend, is the reactionary in the unconventional establishment presided over by her mother, the unorthodox Mme Fisher, who is another of Elizabeth Bowen's dominating women, craving and enjoying power, battening on the weak and the inexperienced. Karen discovers, finally, the extent to which she is involved in the tradition represented by her family and rushes to embrace it; Max Ebhart, her lover and one of Mme Fisher's emotional captives, discovers that his soul belongs to the older woman and that his only means of escaping her is suicide.

The present occurs on a single day in the Fisher home. Purely by happenstance, Naomi and her now bedridden mother have two young visitors: Leopold, son of Karen and the long-dead Max, is to meet his mother for the first time; the other is Henrietta Arbuthnot, two years older than Leopold, who is being kept by the Fishers as a kindness to her aunt in Mentone whom she is traveling to visit en route from England. Henrietta functions chiefly as a means of drawing out Leopold and of providing a contrast to him, particularly in the parallel scenes in which each pays a private visit to Mme Fisher's bedside. The first portion of the book comes to a close when Naomi informs Leopold that, after all, his mother will not be coming to see him. When the present is resumed, the child's stepfather, Ray Forrestier, the man to whom Karen was engaged ten years before, surprisingly arrives in Karen's stead; he spirits the child away rather than have him returned to his foster home in Italy.

Positioned as it is in the novel's structure, part 2 abounds with irony. At every step, as Karen ponders the state of her life and moves unknowingly toward her clandestine assignation, she is exposed; she fatefully surrenders to present feelings, misjudges events within the unfolding action, and shows little thought for the future. But her bedding with Max is not so foolish as it may sound in outline. Unlike several other Bowen heroines, Karen is not a completely naive person; for this reason the situation in which she eventually finds herself is all the more dramatic. The few recorded weeks of her life unfold gradually.

Karen proves a divided young woman whose failure to balance her upbringing and her romantic will leaves her exposed to the recoil of reaction following percipient action. When first met, Karen has just agreed to a lengthy engagement. Her fiancé, Ray, just commencing a career in the diplomatic service, has been posted abroad. Settling back quietly into the safe routine of her parents' Regent's Park home, Karen gradually falls prey to boredom and a growing sense of life passing her by. The extended social goodwill encompassing her engagement and separation from Ray proves oppressive and destructive: "Having to speak of Ray so publicly and constantly began to atrophy private tender thoughts. . . ."[3] Her reaction is one manifestation of the sense of depression she has begun to feel toward the society of which her home is representative, "a world of grace and intelligence," where all unpleasantries are "so many opportunities to behave well" (70). She feels chilled by the fixity of her future—by "the world she sometimes wished to escape from but, through her marriage, meant to inhabit still" (71). As a means of temporary relief, she leaves to visit her Aunt Violet and Uncle Bill in County Cork, "the most unconscious of her relations . . ." (69).

Unexpectedly, Aunt Violet troubles Karen as a person who can hardly be said to have lived. When she says to Karen, "One sometimes wishes one had done more," Karen thinks: "Better to be rooted out hurt, bleeding, alive, like the daisies from the turf, than blow faintly away across the lawn like straw" (85). The passivity of Violet's life becomes more of a shock to Karen when her uncle unintentionally discloses the impending serious operation his wife faces. When Karen senses the nearness of her aunt's death, the tentative defiance Karen has been feeling toward her existence becomes bolder; she tells her aunt: "With Ray I shall be so safe . . . I wish the Revolution would come soon; I should like to start fresh while I am still young, with everything that I had to depend on gone. I sometimes think it is people like us, Aunt Violet, people of consequence, who are unfortunate: we have nothing ahead. I feel it's time something happened" (87). Since Ireland has made her sense of containment even more acute, Karen is relieved to return home.

In London, Karen finds Naomi Fisher. She has come from Paris to settle a legacy, and with her is Max to whom she has just become engaged, much to her mother's disgust. Glad to see Naomi, Karen tries not to meet Max, but she is forced to do so in the face of Naomi's insistence. Karen's reticence stems from the period she had spent as a student in Paris living with the Fisher's, for then she had had a crush on Max, a frequent visitor to Mme Fisher's salon. He had wounded her by his failure to so much as acknowledge her existence. In the light of subsequent events, this early revelation of her instinctive fear of facing the realities of the past and her passion to avoid them is instructive. Moreover, Max's cordiality when they now meet, which contrasts to his previous conduct, carries all the greater impact. Looking back later, Karen and Max realize that Naomi has deliberately engineered their confrontation as a test. At whatever cost to herself, Naomi is prepared to learn the quality of Max's affection before the wedding; her deliberate conduct here, as elsewhere, in proceeding carefully helps the reader judge that of Karen.

Karen's nature rises readily to the strange moodiness of Max. Since he was the first male ever to prompt strong feelings in her, she chooses to read his attention as a continuation or fulfillment of a time when she seemed to herself a more vital, less self-conscious being. Later, after the seduction, she tells him: "I thought you felt as I did, that this finished the past but did not touch the future. Being here does not seem to belong to now, it belongs to the year in Paris when I used to want you so much even to look at me" (171). Fatefully, Max has appeared at a time when Karen craves drama, as this most telling paragraph makes evident:

> She thought, young girls like the excess of any quality. Without knowing, they want to suffer, to suffer they must exaggerate; they like to have loud chords struck on them. Loving art better than life they need men to be actors; only an actor moves them, with his telling smile, undomestic, out of touch with the everyday that they dread. They love to enjoy love as a system of doubts and shocks. They are right: not seeking husbands yet, they have no reason to see love socially. This natural fleshly protest is broken down soon enough; their natural love of the cad is outwitted by their mothers. Vulgarity, inborn like original sin, unfolds with the woman nature, unfolds ahead of it quickly and has a flamboyant flowering in the young girl. (112)

In the weeks following Max's departure from London, Karen asserts her desire to wed Ray, but a new note has now been introduced to her future: "her thoughts had bent strongly to whatever in marriage stays unmapped and dark, with a kind of willing alarm. She had now to look for Max in Ray" (130). Then in succession come a telegram, a letter, and a phone call. The telegram announces the death of Aunt Violet; as with Sydney Warren's graveyard scene in *The Hotel*, the presence of death prompts in Karen not only a sense of transitoriness but the need to grasp life immediately. The letter from Mme Fisher to Mrs. Michaelis is an odd, unexpected one; Karen, pondering over it, puzzled, wonders why it was written. Her astute mother sees the key point (though she too shakes her head at what she takes to be the strange ways of the French). In the letter, Mme Fisher suggests that Max is marrying Naomi simply because of her newly inherited wealth. In her own way, Mme Fisher is beginning to clear the way for an engagement between Karen and Max. When Max then phones Karen proposing a rendezvous in Boulogne, she agrees. In the channel port, Karen learns why Max has called: he tells her that he has heard from Mme Fisher "what [he] dared not think"—namely, that Karen loves him (140). Karen does not deny this, but they both agree they can never marry. Max grants that he needs Naomi; Karen simply decides that she can no longer go through with her marriage to Ray. This decision has the effect of rationalizing the possibilities for her present conduct. When Max tells her that she should go home, that she really does not want adventure, she asks, "Why else am I here?" (155). They then agree on a weekend at Hythe.

Though ample evidence is available, Karen ignores or denies two facts about Max. The first is that Max is in love with her, which she knows for a fact in Hythe. Apprised of it, she says feebly,"I didn't know. . . ." Max answers, "You force me to hide myself," and Karen adds, "If I had known you loved me I would not have dared come" (176). The second fact is that Max is unstable; he himself has been quite insistent about his capacity for erratic behavior. When, in due course, Karen receives the telegram from Naomi reporting Max's suicide, the truth of this instability is fully borne out.

The cause of the suicide stems from Max's realization that he has not escaped the will of Mme Fisher as he had assumed. In her reaction to his news about his affair with Karen, it becomes clear to him that, far from acting independently, he has simply been carrying out her desires. This coincides with the distress he already feels over the troubles Karen faces at home. As Naomi later explains to Karen, "I saw then that Max did not belong to himself. He could do nothing that she had not expected; my mother was at the root of him. I saw that what he had learnt about you and him pleased her, that she had pleasure in it in some terrible way" (194). Naomi then adds that Max was finally crushed by the awareness that "his love for [Karen] had fallen into her hands" (195). Max's only means of escape, his only means of revenge against his captor, was suicide. However, Naomi insists, it was not a calculated but an emotional act—an act of passion.

Her lover gone, Ray in all probability lost, and, with child, Karen tells Naomi: "In ways, you know, Naomi, I should like very much to be ordinary again" (200). Her reaction to her adventure in fact proves total, for, when Mrs. Michaelis dies shortly after the suicide, in effect having been killed by her daughter's conduct, Karen seeks to emulate her completely. When Ray returns, he takes everything in stride and sets aside his diplomatic career for what proves to be a lucrative one in business in order to wed Karen. The child Leopold, the leftover past that Karen no longer wants, finds sanctuary through Naomi's efforts with a wealthy but childless American couple. Whether or not Karen could actually have exorcised the child from her mind is an academic question, since Ray keeps the fact of Leopold's existence alive, not in any way vindictively as a threat held over his wife, but in his recognition that neither Karen nor their marriage can be whole unless she can accept her darker side, and out of a sense of responsibility toward Leopold. Ray's role in this novel parallels that of Cecilia in *To the North* in being the value center. He is solid and sensible, knows that life is never easy, and yet is not without the capacity to act forcefully as his relinquishing of his civil service career indicates. Finally, as his years with Karen demonstrate, he possesses patience. It takes time, but Karen's damaged desire for drama manifests itself once more when she wants to be reunited with her child. But as it is, this desire proves timid. She finds she cannot follow through—which is to say, she lacks the courage and vision to accept a part of herself. Although he cannot be certain of the consequences, Ray can act. Trusting in him, the reader nevertheless suspects that Leopold's ten-year journey toward his Ithaca will succeed, for, at the close, he is like "someone drawing a first breath" (256). Because of his prescience, Ray appears to be what Leopold requires.

Leopold, true son of Max, appears as a high-strung, introspective, complex child. His adjustments to new circumstances, it may be judged, will not be easy, for he is unlike his Paris companion, Henrietta, who is already conscious of adult conduct and of the world as a trying place that must be taken in stride. Ray Forrestier appears, however, to be the man most likely to succeed with Leopold. Hardly wishing to leap out at Leopold on their first evening together, Ray confines his thoughts to himself; they will be expressed soon enough: "(. . . You will notice, we talk where I can talk. You will not quote Mme Fisher, you will not kick me in taxis, you will not shout in houses where they are ill. You will wear a civilized cap, not snub little girls and not get under my feet. There will be many things that you will not like. There are many things that I do not like about you.)" (255–56).

The House in Paris enjoys considerable critical esteem. Artistically, everything introduced into the novel is "used," and it must be granted that the execution fulfills the concept. However, various aspects of the work lead me to rank it lower than other critics. First, the dramatic irony of the second section becomes so repetitive it finally has an adverse effect, for the author appears to be scoring points off her heroine all too easily. Irony employed this relentlessly must yield to a large illumination or prove humanly aggrandizing in order to justify itself. But this irony achieves no such end.

Second, while the characterization of Leopold is quite convincing, far too many pages are devoted to him. He is presumably what the story demands he be—a complex, unhappy child with a troubling mixture of innocence and astuteness. But the points that need to be made regarding him could have been made more succinctly. Clearly Bowen wants him to be taken seriously. When, for example, Naomi comes to take him away from his visit with her mother, she says, "You must come now, at once. I have left you here too long" (223). This remark is intended to carry threats of danger and corruption, but it is hard to be deeply concerned with a nine-year-old who can hardly be credited with comprehending the rebellious philosophy being expounded by Mme Fisher.

And, third, serious doubts must also be raised about the whole relationship between Mme Fisher and Max. It strikes a note of strident melodrama, and it remains an unconvincing solution to the artistic problem of finding a means for Karen to stumble into a painful experience and bear a child. Fourth, and finally, the reader is left with a sense that the author ignored the potentially richest portion of her story in the return of Ray from the East, his subsequent marriage to Karen, and their living "without" Leopold.

There are fine things in the novel, not the least of which are the characterizations of Naomi and Ray. Very near a nonentity in personality, Naomi could have been a flat-stick figure while in fact she is well and humanly realized. And Ray is a minor triumph for Bowen, who is always stronger in creating women. Though his part is small, he comes fully to life.

The Death of the Heart

No Bowen novel has a more comically dramatic opening situation than *The Death of the Heart*. Into the adjusted, unemotional, childless, eight-year marriage of Anna and Thomas Quayne drops Portia, age fifteen, Thomas's half-sister. The Quaynes open the door of their expensive, overly ordered Regent's Park home with little enthusiasm to this newly orphaned child who was conceived in adultery. They are somewhat sustained by the possibility she may be shifted to other relatives after they have had her a year as the elder Mr. Quayne has beseeched them to do. The narrative culminates in a series of shocks: Portia is galvanized into action which, in turn, rebounds upon the Quaynes. By the end of the novel, considerable readjustment at 2 Windsor Terrace seems to be in the offing, and Portia's visit is quite likely a permanent one.

Though much of this "double-stranded" book records Portia's growth and her necessary loss of innocence, the more basic issue is the revitalization, perhaps simply the vitalization, of the moribund marriage. Much of this novel's brilliance results from the skillful blending of these two concerns and their subsidiary matters. This is Elizabeth Bowen's most successful novel, artistically and commercially, and, along with *The Heat of the Day*, it constitutes the peak of her novelistic achievement.

The Quaynes have been living more of an arrangement than a marriage, for each came to it as an emotional cripple. Anna wed on the rebound from the one great love of her life, Robert Pidgeon. Though he dropped her, she has never come to terms with this romantic interlude; she harbors Pidgeon in the recesses of her mind in the same way that she has his letters hidden in a secret drawer of her desk. From her viewpoint, Thomas offered a quiet, undemanding, comfortable marriage, largely because of his passionless nature. Her hopes of establishing a normal role as a mother have long since vanished with her failure to bring her pregnancies to term: her disappointment and her consequent adjustment to childlessness contribute to her stiffness toward Portia. She has settled down to find satisfaction in safe male admirers who can entertain and flatter her but who require no physical reward. Three such bachelors are on the scene during the course of the novel: St. Quentin Martin, an urbane novelist; Eddie, a bright young man employed at Thomas's advertising agency; and latterly, Major Brutt, an older gentleman, a friend of Pidgeon, and recently returned to England out of touch and out of work. As with several other characters in the novel, Anna's appearance belies her inner being, for beneath her brittle sophistication lies an insecure woman who has never risked much for fear of being something less than the best. She is a dabbler.

Thomas originally wed Anna because she was pleasant, self-possessed, and seemingly unconcerned with emotion: in short, she was an ideal marital companion for a man who found the opposite sex a source of anxiety and who abhorred thoughts of intimacy. Marriage for both partners, then, came as a source of relief and as an opportunity to live a quiet life. However, following the ceremony, Thomas experienced the unanticipated; he fell passionately in love with Anna; but assuming her allegiance to their tacit agreement of quietude, he suffers his pent-up feelings privately. In Bowen terms, both are failing to exercise their full emotional potential and will not likely do so unless their current roles are altered. Clearly, this function is to be played by Portia.

The story opens upon Anna and St. Quentin strolling in a winter landscape. She tells him she has been reading Portia's diary, which she came across accidentally, for Portia's record of her days at 2 Windsor Terrace has quite unsettled Anna. It is, she says, "completely distorted and distorting. As I read I thought either this girl or I are mad" (13). Portia has seemingly missed nothing, though "There's certainly not a thing she does not misconstruct" (15). Standing on a bridge in Regent's Park, "their figures sexless and stiff," Anna and her companion watch swans "in slow indignation" swim down cracks in the frozen surface of the lake" (10). Fittingly, Portia becomes associated with bird imagery, and her initial condition is not unlike that of the swans. Because Portia does not learn of Anna's acquaintance with her diary until part 3 of the novel, repercussions do not come until then. Most of part 1 is devoted to characterizing life at Windsor Terrace and to explaining Portia's background.

When Portia's father, the senior Thomas Quayne, was fifty-seven, he had "lost his head completely" and had begun an affair with a woman named Irene, twenty-nine (22). As Anna explains his situation to St. Quentin: "He and [Mrs. Quayne] had married so young—though Thomas, for some reason, was not born for quite a number of years—that he had almost no time to be silly in. Also, I think, she must have hypnotised him into being a good deal steadier than he felt. At the same time she was a woman who thought all men are great boys at heart, and she took every care to keep him one" (13–14).

Mr. Quayne is another instance of retarded adult innocence and of the need, at whatever the risk, for youthful excess. When Irene becomes pregnant, Mr. Quayne tells his wife, and "Mrs. Quayne [is] quite as splendid as ever . . ." (23). She becomes "all heroic reserve," calms her husband, packs him off to Irene, starts divorce proceedings, and settles down to enjoy her house and garden in contented peace. Like hopeless babies, Mr. Quayne and his bride retire to the south of France and begin a wandering existence in cheap hotels. He suffers because the growing Portia has no proper life, and during a trip to London, he secretly inspects Windsor Terrace and envisions his daughter sharing the normal family life it suggests to him. After he dies, Portia and her mother continue the transient existence, but, when Irene suddenly dies after an operation, Portia becomes her father's legacy to Regent's Park.

An inside view of the Quayne affair is provided by an older servant, Matchett, who had worked for Thomas's mother before coming to Anna along with her mother-in-law's good furniture when she had died. Matchett, stolid and humorless, but Portia's only source of affection, makes a distinction between the right action and the good one. In her view, Mrs. Thomas Quayne "meant to do right" (95). She explains to Portia, "Sacrificers . . . are not the ones to pity. The ones to pity are those that they sacrifice" (90). She has been a great admirer of Portia's father who, in her estimation, was unlike his wife in being honest and natural. She views Mrs. Quayne as a role player who was prepared to maintain her concept of herself at whatever cost to anyone else. In the light of Matchett's views, we see that Thomas and Anna are also doing the "right" rather than the good thing by Portia.

This background detail helps to account for Anna's report that she and Portia "are on such curious terms—when I ever do take a line, she never knows what it is" (11). Quite evidently, feelings must come to replace manners. That Portia, however, has two left feet because of her inexperience is humorously brought out in scenes at her private school for girls where she is decidedly unsuccessful in coping with the established decorum: "she had not learnt that one must learn . . ." (65). Small wonder she feels all of London threatening her:

> She had watched life, since she came to London, with a sort of despair—motivated and busy always, always progressing: even people pausing on bridges seemed to pause with a purpose; no bird seemed to pursue a quite aimless flight. The spring of the works seemed unfounded only by her. . . . She could not believe there was not a

plan of the whole set-up in every head but her own . . . nothing was not weighed down by significance. In her home life (her new home life) with its puzzles, she saw dissimulation always on guard; she asked herself humbly for what reason people said what they did not mean, and did not say what they meant. She felt most certain to find the clue when she felt the frenzy behind the clever remark. (72–73)

Having a modest relationship with Anna and Thomas, and a closer but milder one with Matchett, Portia grabs rather eagerly at the interest shown in her by the irresponsible Eddie. From the viewpoint of the contemporary British novel, Eddie is an interesting creation because he so evidently anticipates Kingsley Amis's protagonist in *Lucky Jim*; for, like Jim Dixon, Eddie comes from a modest background and is seeking to locate himself in the establishment, in which he does not believe. A very conscious role player, Eddie prefigures Jim Dixon in his habits of face-making and mimicry.

The relationship between Portia and Eddie is undemandingly comfortable from his viewpoint. He takes joy in her childlike innocence, and he feels she is the one person with whom he need not assume an interminable pose. Eddie, as it develops, misjudges in assuming that Portia will place no demands upon him. Really a very self-centered being, he is concerned with his welfare and personal freedom, but his surface superciliousness really cloaks despair. An "experienced innocent," Eddie bears a resemblance to Emmeline of *To the North* in his unwillingness to adjust to the non-Edenic facts of life, or at least in his unwillingness to adjust without exacting his own price from the world. He seeks to punish and to travesty love because it cannot be what he longs for it to be; he sees only himself as reality since he is the only person he is prepared to trust. Portia, from his viewpoint, is really a new lease on the impossible life; with her, he seeks to sustain the innocence of adolescent love, the state that holds out to him the possibility of beautiful fulfillment so long as it is never tested. Portia, of course, has no such insight as his; but she discovers soon enough Eddie's unwillingness to allow their affair to progress, and she is left pondering his distress over her unwillingness to sustain their status quo and her desire to grow up.

Part 2, "The Flesh," shifts to a contrasting setting, one that offers Portia an alternate kind of life with its own range of new characters and experiences. Anna, feeling the need of a vacation, whisks Thomas to Capri; Portia is sent to the seaside at Seale to live with Anna's one-time governess, the widowed Mrs. Heccomb and her two working step-children, Dickie and Daphne. Home is called Wakiki (which is intended to give this sequence overtones of undemanding, irresponsible Pacific Island life), and the household is the antithesis of the highly mannered Windsor Terrace. Wakiki is sustained by blasting radios and by conversation conducted by shouting above them; all is "pushing and frank," though neurotically proper. Portia discovers "the upright rudeness of the primitive state—than which nothing is more rigid" (207). Life at Windsor Terrace is "edited," but that at Wakiki is the reverse. The contrast recalls that between the stately home in *The Last September* and the huts of the army families.

More at home at Wakiki but still reticent, Portia falls in with the crowd presided over by Daphne and Dickie. Portia soon becomes anxious to invite Eddie for a weekend, and Mrs. Heccomb, assured that Eddie is well known to Anna, assumes his visit will be quite proper. Portia awaits his coming anxiously, for she has decided on the reality of Seale and wishes him to confirm it for her. Eddie has hardly arrived, however, before he declares it "unreal," for in his self-conscious state he is well aware Wakiki is the unexamined life. The only member of the Seale crowd who is at all introspective, Cecil, is barely tolerated—is considered ineffectual and is labeled "a cissie."

Unknowingly betrayed in London by Anna, Portia is to know betrayal in Seale through Eddie. Sitting between Portia and Daphne at a Saturday night movie, Eddie ends up, as Portia discovers, holding Daphne's hand. Since Eddie has been introduced into the crowd as Portia's friend, she finds this experience painful. When she is alone with Eddie the next day, she challenges his conduct. The episode, he explains, is innocent enough in his view and was intended to lead to nothing further, but this view is not easily conveyed to Portia. In fairness to Eddie, it must be said that he has warned Portia not to get serious with him and to make demands: "Never *be* potty about me: I can't do anything for you" (256). Furthermore, Eddie anticipates what St. Quentin later elaborates for Portia when he says, "Don't you know how dreadful the things you say are?" (257).

In her diary Portia views Seale to London's disadvantage: "In London I do not know what anybody is doing, there are no things I can watch people do. Though things have hurt me since I was left behind here, I would rather stay with the things here than go back to where I do not know what will happen" (274). Even Portia feels the great temptation of comfort, of seeking out an effortless stasis. However, she must return to London to be greeted by Matchett, who observes, "I can't see that this change has done you harm. Nor the shakeup either; you were getting too quiet" (280).

When Thomas and Anna return, it is evident they have not changed. Having been greeted warmly by Portia in the front hall, Anna cannot wait to go up to her bath, and Thomas, claiming a headache, quickly vanishes into his study. Later, Thomas observes to Anna, "Portia gave us a welcome," to which she replies, "It was we who were not adequate." But Anna remains prepared with her justifications: "let's face it—whoever is adequate? We all create situations each other can't live up to, then break our hearts at them because they don't" (289). This statement proves a telling one in the light of ensuing action. Though aware of their inadequacy in dealing with Portia, the Quaynes seem prepared to let matters drift. In the Bowen world, they are riding for an upset.

Critics generally agree that the "devil" of the final section is St. Quentin since he imparts to Portia the "forbidden" knowledge that Anna has been reading her diary. However, the devil may more properly be viewed as a situation rather than a person, for a comment Major Brutt makes to Anna provides the clue: "that's the devil, you know, about not having a fixed address" (315). This statement assesses the root of the trouble, for what Portia ultimately feels is a lack of any sense of permanency. Her efforts at the close are directed toward finding a sanctuary, and, in a rather roundabout manner, she probably succeeds.

After learning from St. Quentin of Anna's having read the diary, Portia telephones Eddie to tell him, and he in turn calls Anna. Although his position with both Thomas and Anna is insecure, Eddie conveys his displeasure. When five days later, Portia arrives home to find Anna and Eddie tête-à-tête over tea, she is convinced they have been talking and laughing together about her. Two days later, when Portia walks out on Windsor Terrace, the time lapse, observes the narrator, is "long enough for the sense of two allied betrayals to push up a full growth, like a double tree . . ." (327). Portia leaves her home after having arranged to meet Eddie, and, unbeknownst to him, she is intent on living with him. After Eddie has been more or less forced into taking her to his apartment and after he has reiterated his earlier claim that she does not know the ropes and has "a completely lunatic set of values" and that he simply cannot risk harboring her, she departs prepared to play her final card. She goes to Major Brutt, tells him she has "nowhere to be," and informs the poor dazed man that she wishes to marry him. She rather cruelly seeks to enlist him as an ally by telling him that Anna also laughs at him. When he insists that he must call Windsor Terrace, Portia tells him that Thomas and Anna will not know what to do, and she instructs him to say that her return will depend on their doing "the right thing."

Meanwhile, Portia's absence has been noted by the Quaynes and St. Quentin, their dinner guest. The air is already tense, and Anna and Thomas have already begun unburdening themselves to each other when the Major's call comes. Thomas now learns about the diary, and the scene that this disclosure threatens is just barely avoided as they turn their attention to the question of "the right thing." They quickly enough reject any thoughts of having

Portia come across town alone in a taxi or of her being escorted home by Major Brutt. The importance of the issue they do not doubt. Anna points out: "It's not simply a question of getting her home this evening; it's a question of all three going on living here . . . yes, this is a situation. She's created it" (371).

When St. Quentin initiates an important train of thought by suggesting that Anna and Thomas "are both unnaturally conscious of [Portia] . . ." (372), Anna seeks to put herself in Portia's place and to express what her feelings must be: "Frantic, frantic desire to be handled with feeling, and, at the same time, to be let alone. Wish to be asked how I felt, great wish to be taken for granted—" (377). The right act, really the good act, the natural thing, they decide is "something quite obvious. Something with no fuss" (375). When Portia is normally brought home, Matchett brings her; so they dispatch Matchett and also decide against calling Major Brutt. Thomas says, "This is a *coup* or nothing" (377).

Bowen implies in her closing passage that life at Windsor Terrace will be better, but she once more avoids suggesting any miraculous change. Anna has already shown a humanitarian side, one that Portia is unaware of, in her efforts to find employment for Major Brutt, whose worth she recognizes. And she has also and most importantly come to terms with her harbored past feelings for Pidgeon. She admits to herself, as she never previously has, and tells Major Brutt as much, that Pidgeon did not really care for her, that their affair came to nothing because neither trusted the other. And she and Thomas have talked, as Thomas earlier complained they never did. Having "saved" Portia by pulling her back from a speeding car on one of their recent strolls in the park, he now appears committed to saving her in another sense. Emphasized at the very close, and clearly intended to contrast with the frigid landscape of the opening, is a description of the spring evening with its "intimation of summer coming . . ." (384). And the piano music issuing from an open window as the curtain falls hints at the new harmony seemingly to be realized at Windsor Terrace.

Many factors contribute to the success of *The Death of the Heart*. Never did the author find a more richly dramatic situation. Perhaps she was never so close to many facets of her own life. Ultimately, though, the book's stature relates to the narrator. It is to her ultimately that we respond. This manifests itself most immediately in the comic vision recording and commenting upon a sequence of delicious confrontations. What the novel offers through the narrator is the pattern for a mature and fully realized human consciousness. All of the characters, ideally, should aspire toward the narrator's totality of awareness, perception, humor, compassion, and, finally, style.

Chapter Four
The Power of the Past

> Remember that all our failures
> are ultimately failures in love.
> —Iris Murdoch, *The Bell*

Elizabeth Bowen's third group and final four novels disclose her readiness to set herself new and challenging problems. In part, of course, she had to move on from *The Death of the Heart*, which carried her earlier material to a finely realized logical conclusion. Aside from this novel, her last work is in many ways her most interesting; for it shows the author working with a new sense of adventure. And, if none of these novels quite match the perfection of *The Death of the Heart*, they reflect the touch of a poised and knowing craftsman. *The Heat of the Day* (1949) is the most ambitious of her novels; *A World of Love* (1955) and *The Little Girls* (1964), her most intellectually intricate; and *Eva Trout* (1969), the most bizarre.

The Heat of the Day, set chiefly in wartime London, aims to make a major statement about the conditions preceding and fomenting World War II. In addition to being a professed "big" novel, it is Bowen's most daring one. As such, it has vulnerable aspects some critics have readily noted. In this novel, as in no other, the characters function symbolically; they stand for classes of people and social tendencies as Bowen saw them function between the wars and fulfill themselves in the Holocaust. In outline, the central love triangle, composed of a woman who has abdicated the artistocratic responsibilities of her class and two men who are a spy and a counterspy, appears improbable and melodramatic. But, if the threesome is viewed as moving through the dense wartime milieu with its pervasive sense of exaggeration and unexpectedness, the improbability is lessened. The heroine, in spite of the significance she must bear, is possibly the best realized one in the author's gallery.

A World of Love is the one instance in which Bowen's style assumes a disproportionate importance. The verbal preciousness is distracting, if not finally destructive, since it creates difficulties of comprehension that are out of all proportion to the weight of the subject matter. Like *To the North*, *Friends and Relations*, and *The House in Paris*, this novel is a work with parts rather than a whole piece. Considered in conjunction with *The Last September* and *The Death of the Heart*, however, *A World of Love* affords an interesting combination and a reworking of previous material toward a new realization. It shares with *The Last September* an Irish setting and insights into the Irish character; like *The Death of the Heart*, it employs more than one heroine. As a literary performance, *A World of Love* is clever, but to make an additional claim for it is difficult.

The Little Girls, like *The Heat of the Day*, is symbolic, but it differs in the degree of ambivalence attached to its symbols. Consequently, this novel is Bowen's most challenging book; this fact is all the more surprising in the light of its taut and racy style. We might conceivably be reminded of Wallace Stevens's poetry with its pure, crystalline exterior and its metaphysical interior. In this novel, the author presents what must constitute the ultimate variation upon her innocent heroine character by creating one who is sixty-one years old.

By virtue of their emphasis on the past as it impinges upon the present, these three novels constitute a group. The topic has always interested Bowen, but it is one she had not previously dealt with so pervasively or so radically. Compared with her other books, these three quite simply encompass more time since most of the principal characters are older: those in *The Heat of the Day* are around forty; those in *A World of Love*, over fifty; the women in *The Little Girls*, in their sixties.

These books emphasize that the quality of an individual's life is significantly influenced by his attitude to his accrued memories and experiences. Characters in each of the stories are shown in the midst of life as acting upon distorted and delimiting recollections, and they are forced by circumstances to confront this fact. Thus they are afforded an opportunity for reassessment and readjustment toward a more vital existence.

Eva Trout is somewhat apart in arriving at a negative conclusion. It too shares a concern for the past, but the heroine, rendered permanently inept by a careless upbringing and burdened with inherited wealth, is unable to gain self-knowledge or an achieved life. The author's last novel is both grotesque and dark.

The Heat of the Day

Elizabeth Bowen's one attempt at the big novel, *The Heat of the Day*, is her most powerful one, but it is not so perfectly realized as *The Death of the Heart*. Nonetheless, these remain as the twin peaks of her work. Described as both a war novel and a love story, the novel is either only in a limited sense.

The impact of the war, particularly the bombing of the civilian population of London in 1942, is tellingly rendered. But Bowen is not interested in the war per se; rather, it is presented as the logical culmination of the between-the-wars wasteland. The war, then, while vividly real, an undeniable actuality, moves imagistically beyond actual history.

Prewar conditions, conveyed through the lives of a handful of characters, are analogous with the social situation in any other Bowen novel—situations that, as previously noted, have their own counterforce built into them. As one character observes, "Dunkirk was waiting there in us . . ." (263). With a situation so radical as a war, it is not feasible to postulate recovery for the generation for whom the landscape of blitz is an inevitable inheritance; with the war comes an exhilarating release from the torpidity of the wasteland, but the forces of shock, having to be extreme, are largely self-destructive. In a book, however, which regards the war as a social watershed, it is appropriate that there be the subsidiary theme of the fresh start and that it be expressed through members of the new generation who will inherit a world cleansed by the massive convulsion.

No Bowen novel suffers more from story summary than this one; indeed, some of its melodrama is bound to sound incredible. But, as we have observed, the heightened wartime atmosphere helps absorb the unusual incidents. Few readers would deny the author gains a "willing suspension of disbelief." The central story revolves around Stella Rodney, a handsome woman in her forties; her lover Robert Kelway; and her would-be lover, Harrison, a skulking counterspy. Stella is a relatively normal character, but the two men are aberrations. Stella and Robert, both engaged in secret government work, have been in love for two years. Harrison, a man Stella has met only once previously, contacts her claiming urgent business and comes to her flat. He has two pieces of information and a proposition to make her: first, Robert Kelway is passing information to the enemy; second, only he, Harrison, knows this fact. His proposition is quite to the point: if Stella will become his mistress he will not report Robert. Clearly, this situation has all the makings of a Graham Greene novel with its usual atmosphere of seediness, but Bowen's treatment is quite different. The reader is surprised that Stella's reaction to Harrison is not considerably sharper than it is. But not until near the end of the novel will the reader come to understand the calmness of her response. Quite obviously the book begins with very strong appeals to the reader's curiosity. The odd nature of Harrison, the truth of his accusations, and Stella's reaction are all to be wondered at.

Early commentators recognized the relationship of *The Heat of the Day* to E. M. Forster's *Howards End*. In his novel, Forster draws into contact representatives of the three broad classes of English society: Margaret Schlegel, middle class; Henry Wilcox, upper class; and Leonard Bast, lower class. Bowen offers Stella and her son Roderick as representatives of the upper class; Harrison and Robert of the middle; and, the principal character of an important subplot, Louie Lewis, of the lower. In a comparison of the two novels, William Heath makes this most useful observation: "the distance between their final attitudes can suggest a great deal about the forty-year period that separates [them]."[1]

For Forster, the Schlegels represent the hope for a healthy society, the responsible balance between the "prose" of public demands (the overly abstract Henry) and the "poetry" of private need (the overly subjective Leonard). Dealing with a situation that is fait accompli, Bowen places the responsibility for chaos upon the middle class, represented by the Kelway family. Her treatment of the Rodneys is dualistic; Stella must share in the blame for war because she largely abdicated the responsibilities of her class, but Roderick, in planning to modernize the estate he inherits in Ireland, carries hope into the future. And Louie, too, with her new baby and her own form of courage and integrity, is to be a source of strength in the new order.

The one piece of literature, however, permeating the book is *Hamlet*. Bowen could hardly have selected allusions to another work to underline more readily the heavy, black atmosphere that hangs over much of *The Heat of the Day*. There is much to remind one of the drama: Stella, long involved in self-debate; Harrison, on his first appearance, looming up from amid tombstones; parents guilty by virtue of selfishness; a mad woman speaking sense; a trip across water leading to action; Roderick ready, at the close, to take command. It is obvious there is something "rotten in the state," and there are allusions to the times being out of joint.

Several weeks pass before Stella confronts Robert with her information. Robert denies it. Shortly thereafter, Harrison tells Stella he knows she has spoken to Robert, and he rather convincingly pinpoints the very night because Robert has altered the pattern of his behavior just as Harrison predicted he would when he became aware he was being watched. In the penultimate chapter Robert admits the truth of Harrison's claim and seeks to justify his actions to Stella before he either slips or falls to his death from the roof of her apartment house. Previous to this admission of guilt, he has taken Stella to his home, Holme Delme, and, through her contact with his mother and his sister, Ernestine, she acquires a context for his final disclosures. The Holme Delme sequence contains the most castigating satire of the Bowen oeuvre.

Among Mrs. Kelway's antecedents are the father in Katherine Mansfield's "The Daughters of the Late Colonel," and, perhaps even more directly, the loathsome "Grannie" of D. H. Lawrence's *The Virgin and the Gypsy.* Such descriptive phrases as "diamond-like" and "ice-blue" have a particularly Lawrencean ring. Mrs. Kelway has dominated her home, has crushed her husband, and has sought to mold her children to her dehumanized sense of life. The sign at the entrance to the Holme Delme driveway is, "Caution Hidden Drive." Mr. Kelway, now dead, clearly was never taken seriously or permitted any self-expression; he was "only nominally allowed the fiction of being" the master.

Within her living room, Mrs. Kelway sits knitting (the fate of the nation?), and she is protected or withdrawn behind a series of screens. She is a version of the stereotyped Queen Victoria loftily stating "we are not amused." Stella quickly discovers the impossibility of conversation with her, for Mrs. Kelway is conscious only of what she herself says. Willful and inhuman, she is characterized by the imagery of the hunt and war: "decoy," "strategic," "command." To Stella, she is "wicked," and what is most frightening is the indication that she is not unique but simply representative of a whole race of women. She is the solidification of a type that is life-denying and power conscious. The whole niggling, self-righteous, self-asserting approach to existence is captured in the great fuss over three pennies for Stella in order for her to mail a letter for Mrs. Kelway when she returns to London. Stella is appalled.

It is supremely ironic that this woman who spouts such comments as, "I have never thought of what I wanted," and "It is not a question of happiness," should be known as "Muttikins" (250). Suffering a self-conceived martyrdom, Mrs. Kelway is determined that hell shall be everyone's fate—and achieves her wish with the war. Robert, dispirited at his deepest level, says, "I was born wounded; my father's son" (263). In his room, Stella find the walls lined with dozens of photographs of Robert at all ages and in all of the appropriate poses: with the great black dog, smiling in white flannels, standing next to a bright, attractive young woman, and so forth. He has not created a life; he has simply stepped into the prearranged poses. Robert tells Stella, "Each time I come back again into it I'm hit in the face by the feeling that I don't exist . . ." (112). He is one of the "ruined boys" W. H. Auden speaks of in "Consider." The only communication in his home is in a "dead language" that gives rise to "repression, doubts, fears, subterfuges, and fibs" (247).

A fine touch is the fact that Mrs. Kelway and her daughter provide wartime sanctuary for two children. Mrs. Kelway likes to remind her son that she has taken the children "when it was not convenient . . ." (241). The situation is forcefully poignant viewed through the eyes of the girl Anne: "Never a heartbeat; never the light disregarding act, the random word or spontaneous kiss; never laughter . . . anger always in a smoulder. . . . Though she did not know it, she had never seen anyone being happy . . ." (254).

Robert has achieved a profound insight into the force of the middle-class power: "What else but an illusion could have such power?" (116). It is the nature of reality to reveal flaws, sooner or later, but these can be circumvented by the make-believe of self-importance and appropriateness. Lies, because they are total abstractions, are always true. But, whatever he has become, Robert has escaped being another Ernestine who, "rather like a dog," enjoys greater pleasure with a dog than with another human being, and whose face contains an "absense of human awareness" that is to Stella "quite startling" (102).

By revolting, Robert has avoided her fate, but the great danger in reaction is always overreaction. Bowen characterizes Robert's siding with dictatorial powers as "romanticism fired once too often" (268). The final straw for Robert, so far as his society is concerned, was Dunkirk, where he was wounded. Apparently, he had gone to war seeing it as a sign of new hope, but after watching the "army of freedom queuing up to be taken off by pleasure boats," he was finished with England (263). One of the book's sad paradoxes is that his assertion of individuality rewarded him with a rich love affair this very assertion foredoomed.

Bowen is careful to present Robert as a revolutionary rather than as a Nazi sympathizer, for, if he is anti-England, he is not pro-German. The reader, along with Stella, sees Robert before his death not so much as a traitor but as a corrupt human who seized upon an unfortunate doctrine. He is a man who has chosen to rise above or to ignore nationalism: "there are no more countries left," he says, though telling Stella she is his country (258). What he seeks is change and the elimination of "the muddled, mediocre, damned" (259). Like his card-carrying fellow travelers pursued by McCarthyism in America a decade later, Robert has given up on democracy where people are "kidded along from cradel to grave" (259). The Nazis are, for him, in the position most likely to accomplish the ends he desires; they are destroyers, if not builders. Muddle has left him desiring the clear and simple, and in Nazism he sees order. Stella can sympathize up to a point with Robert, but she can see that he has a greatly oversimplified worldview and that he has lost sight of humanity in his own negative drive. There is reason to believe Bowen sees Hitler as simply a manifestation of the Kelway way of life, and she believes that he rose to power on the backs of Germany's counterparts to the Kelways. At one point she characterizes the twists and turns of life in the upstairs of Holme Delme as "swastika-arms" (249). And there are also suggestions that Harrison's work is not unlike that of the Gestapo, implying that both combatants are alike. Thus, the novel is disclosing not simply the nature of England but the troubles underlying all of Europe or the Western world.

To turn to Harrison is not, surprisingly, to move away from Robert. Near the end of the novel, Harrison tells Stella his Christian name is Robert. Robert and Harrison are thus mirror images—the one postulates the other. If the one has had too much home, the other has had too little. If Robert has yielded to much of himself to the private will, Harrison has dehumanized himself through submission to the public will. Throughout, Bowen has hinted at the links between the men. Before he leaves her flat to die, Robert hears Stella explain that Harrison has him "at heart" (274). Only Robert justifies and provides Harrison with an identity. Privately, Harrison admits liking the war because it gives him a stature he otherwise lacks.

Little of Harrison's past is disclosed, but this lack indicates the point: he is rootless man. Stella appeals to him not as a source of passion but as a gracious woman with the ability to create a warm home; he seems happier with her flat than with her, and he is never more pleased than when she asks him to bring her a glass of milk from the kitchen. Indeed, he rather pathetically tells her that, for him, her flat is home. Since Robert can give Stella his heart but not his mind, it follows that Harrison's attachment to Stella is essentially in his mind; he cannot give her his heart, for, indeed, he may not have one to give. After Robert's death, he comes to visit Stella in her new flat. She rejects him, and he accepts this rejection "with relief" (311).

By this time, Stella has succumbed to exhaustion, all feeling spent. As she and Harrison sit talking, while an air raid is in progress, she tells him she may marry. When he tells her she owes it to her future husband to seek shelter, she denies it matters—love or death, she will take her chances. She accepts her role as a child of her times, and she knows she shares in the corruption of her generation. When, years ago, her husband, ironically named Victor, had returned wounded from World War I, he shocked her by claiming she did not love him and had departed to live with the nurse who had cared for him. He no sooner had gained a divorce when he died.

At that time, her whole sorry travail of dislocation and doomed love had begun. Victor's family believes that Stella had provoked the divorce, and she has said nothing to deny it, preferring, as she tells Harrison, to appear a monster rather than a fool. Roderick, reared believing this of his mother, had learned the truth from Cousin Nettie, and had confronted his mother with it. Admitting the truth, she had asserted that its revelation came too late: "Whatever has been buried, surely, corrupts . . ." (220). She admits to Harrison, finally, that "there's an underside to me that I've hated, that you almost make me like . . ." (219). In the simplest terms, then, the main story of *The Heat of the Day* is the failure on a grand scale of feeling.

This being so, it is proper to discover in the characters Roderick and Louie a new purity and honesty of feeling. Roderick surprises his mother with his interest in his ailing Cousin Nettie and in hopes and plans he makes for his land in Ireland. The brief Irish passage appears as a momentary picture of sanity in an otherwise blighted world, and it is there that word of Montgomery's victory comes. Roderick, apparently, will find his roots in the remote rather than the recent past, and, in so doing, he will attach himself to a tradition of stability.

Louie, for her part, suggests the human capacity to endure, to withstand confusion, distortion, and disaster without losing her desire for basic domestic values. Left a war widow with a baby son, she is determined he will have a happy home, and her hard-won achievement of wisdom seems to assure it. Hers is the final vision of the future, the enduring grace and beauty of the three swans.

The Heat of the Day is a prime illustration of a novel whose parts, being greater than the whole, are sufficient to make a work distinguished in spite of evident weaknesses. Some of its scenes are among the author's most memorable—the opening one in Regent's Park, Stella at Cousin Francis's funeral, Stella visiting Mount Morris, Roderick visiting Nettie, Louie with her friend Connie, and the meal in the underground restaurant. And the chief glories, of course, are the vivid descriptions of London under the blitz. No other novel gave the author more trouble than this one. We may intuit why this was so while acknowledging its justification.

A World of Love

After her wartime fiction and *The Demon Lover* (1945) story collection in particular, Elizabeth Bowen could hardly have been expected to return untouched by the increased sense of psychic aberration the blitz and the buzz bombs gave to her more normal concerns—to such typical themes as hurt feelings and young love in a family situation—as she does in *A World of Love*. The connection between this novel and *The Heat of the Day* is rather explicit since Bowen's opening sentence represents something of an in-joke, "The sun rose on a landscape still pale with the heat of the day before."[2] Though this novel is an experiment that was not successful and is, consequently, one of Bowen's least satisfactory books, it is interesting for several reasons. Among the foremost of these is its similarity to her earliest novels, *The Hotel* and *The Last September*. Like them, it has a beautiful girl in a relatively confined world whose instinctual quest for womanhood transmits shock waves that generally enlarge to the circumference of her sphere, but these narrative basics become transmuted into a fascinating variation through both the configurative and the verbal creations of the author's increasingly metaphysical approach. In *A World of Love*, Jane Danby, twenty, with "a face perfectly ready to be a woman's, but not yet so," and her sister Maud, twelve, whose "unmistakable content was moral force," become the instruments that harrow their home (11, 171). Jane has just returned from completing an English education paid for by her Aunt Antonia, who has accompanied her home on one of her frequent sojourns. Home is Montefort, owned by Antonia, a small, Irish country manor, and it is presided over by Lilia Danby and farmed by her husband Fred, Antonia's illegitimate cousin.

Not unexpectedly, the book opens with Montefort in a moribund state. It is "half-sleep," and "The door no longer knew hospitality . . ." (9). Conditions have actually been thus for twenty years, and at the root of the trouble is the former owner, Guy. Details from the past that account for the unsatisfactory lives and relationships of the elder Danbys are released throughout the novel. Antonia, her cousin Guy, and Fred, the "by-blow," have grown up at Montefort. Gifted with tremendous vitality, Antonia and Guy have lived something of a Wuthering Heights existence. Fred recalls, "You and he were something out of the common. . . . The way you two were, you could have run the world" (120).

By the time World War I began and Guy had joined the army, Antonia had fallen in love with him, but, during the course of one of his leaves, he had become engaged to an English girl, Lilia, then seventeen. By the time Guy had departed for the last time to France in 1918, he had acquired another woman, a fact known by both Antonia and Lilia, who have yet to meet. Not until the end of the novel do the two women bring this information into the open. As the narrator eventually observes, Guy "had stirred up too much; he had scattered round him more promises as to some dreamed-of extreme of being than one man could have hoped to live to honour" (145).

After Guy's death in battle, Antonia inherits Montefort and decides to do something for Lilia. This decision, in retrospect, appears unfortunate, for "never had intervention proved more fatal" (18); the narrator suggests that Lilia would have been better left alone. At any rate, when, after ten years, Lilia remains unwed, Antonia feels justified in taking matters into her own hands. She tells Fred, who has been drifting about, that she will turn Montefort over to him for a share in the profits if he will marry Lilia. An obvious admirer of Guy, Fred agrees that "Guy's girl" is worth a look. The wedding takes place, though not until Antonia has threatened Lilia with the withdrawal of additional assistance if she refuses.

When Jane is seven, her mother bolts for London and announces she will not return. Once more Antonia threatens her; and, after softening her, Antonia dispatches Fred to bring her home. Fred's wooing succeeds, they return, and the reunion is marked by the conception of Maud. Since all of these events precede the story proper, it should be evident that *A World of Love* is burdened with more exposition than any other Bowen novel. However, while all of this information helps explain why Montefort is not a happy home, it does not fully account for the present states of the adults. These states are implied as the present action—the reactive action for which Montefort is more than due—unfolds.

While rummaging around in the attic, Jane finds, or, as the narrator views it, is found by, a bundle of love letters. The letters were written by Guy while he was at Montefort to an unknown person. A ready recipient for romance, Jane becomes enamored of them. When Guy writes, "I wish you were," Jane can cry, "I am!" Not unexpectedly the letters have considerable impact on the whole house, revivifying thoughts of Guy especially for Antonia and Lilia. The letters create tensions for three emotionally intense days (the countryside, meanwhile, is suffering prostrating heat), at the end of which they are burned by a wiser Jane, symbolically releasing the omnipresent Guy, and conditions at Montefort have altered obviously for the better.

What gradually emerges is the extent of Guy's impact upon these people. Having been dazzled by his tremendous energy, they have never truly comprehended his death, which explains why the narrator sees him as a presence rather than as a ghost. It might be assumed he has remained as a force in their memories, but this is not the case: "not memories was it but expectations which haunted Montefort. His immortality was in their longings, while each year mocked the vanishing garden" (145). Guy's contemporaries are never unaware that "The living [are] living in his life-time. . . . They were incomplete" (65). Living in these terms consists in enduring a timeless limbo.

Perhaps Lilia's waiting is the most strained of all, for her whole existence as Guy's intended ("if not the Beloved, what was Lilia?") is frozen in a state of suspension. Like Stella in *The Heat of the Day*, Lilia has lived a lie—as if she preferred, like Stella, to be a monster rather than a fool in her own eyes, although this cognition implies more self-awareness on her part than the text allows. It is more accurate to say she has never really permitted herself to confront the truth, for, once a true reassessment of Guy begins to take place, she can admit to herself that "not till today had she wholly taken account. Guy was dead, and only today at dinner had she sorrowed for him" (72).

For her part, Antonia has acted as if it were necessary to keep everything going, to keep Guy's world intact until his return. Her relationship with Lilia appears as almost the only noteworthy event of her life, or of their lives: "Thrown together, they had adhered: virtually, nothing more than this had happened to them since their two girlhoods" (74). Much of her time literally consists of putting in time, sleeping late, drinking alone, napping, lying on the beach. Antonia's sharpness and bossiness are those of a person bored and expecting to stay so (interestingly, she calls the vital Jane "a bore").

Fred, the man caught in the middle, is aware that he is Guy's substitute and that, as such, he has hardly been fairly regarded for himself. He, of course, knows nothing of yet another woman. Of the three, he is the only one who has sought to remain somewhat vital—if the rumors of Irish lasses down the lane are true. Denied the proper role of man of the family, as Maud takes occasion to indicate to Antonia, he has channeled himself into hard work.

Jane, Lilia, and Antonia all experience the same doubts when they begin to emerge from their respective states of illusion; they cannot be certain of their immediate direction. Lilia thinks, "What had now happened must either kill her or, still worse, force her to live . . ." (72). The ludicrous situation of seeing the beautiful Jane having her first love affair with a packet of letters brings both Lilia and Jane up short. Officially, the fiction that the letters rightfully belong to Lilia persists to the close, but she and Antonia know otherwise and, in the end, so too does Jane. Lilia's first active response to the sense of change in the air is to have her hair cut in the recent style, which represents a return to an earlier day when bobbing and shingling were fashionable.

But this symbolic attempt to retrieve time results in an unexpected confrontation. While Lilia is sitting alone in the Montefort garden, she suddenly senses the approach of someone—she is certain that it is Guy—when in walks Fred. He, it appears, was and is her destiny. He has brought her the letters, which he has taken from Maud who had taken them from under the rock where they had been hidden (abandoned?) by Jane, in the belief that they are hers. Lilia is touched by his act, and the next thing Montefort witnesses is their driving off together for a spin in the old Danby Ford. When Lilia later admits to Antonia that she knew of Guy's other woman, her settlement with the past is complete, and her emergence as a "new woman" seems assured.

It is Maud who starts Jane on her road to awareness and who provides the finishing touches to Antonia's emergence as a more sympathetic being. Traversing the thigh-high bracken along the river, enfolded in a romantic mood, Jane is suddenly accosted by Maud, who yells, first, "What are *you* playing?"

and, then, "What are you pretending about that tree?" (70–71). These questions are sufficient to make Jane feel foolish and recognize the silliness of her affair with Guy. She is now ready for a second test, and this comes in the form of a real letter from the nouveau riche English woman who has recently purchased the local castle. Vesta Latterly, having earlier spotted Jane and thinking the girl's beauty would be an adornment at her table, invites her to a dinner party. While *A World of Love* largely concerns itself with the dangers of past events, it also presents a counterstatement about the poise and sense of responsibility a past can bestow—a lesson Jane learns at the castle. And a lesson she needs to learn, since, daughter of Montefort, she has "an instinctive aversion from the past . . . a sort of pompous imposture . . ." (48).

The Latterly world proves phantasmagoric. Vesta's circle is comprised of hulks who have surrendered their soul to Mamon—as Jane recognizes. An older Irishman comparing the past and present tells her, "These days, one goes where the money is—with all due respect to this charming lady. Those days, we went where the people were" (94). Jane knows Guy often frequented the castle, and, when there is an empty place at the table, she imagines him present, not now as her lover, but as her ancestor from a nobler time. Though tipsy with her first martini, she can see that Guy is more real than those present, for, as old Terrance has told her, "You can't buy the past" (93). Jane's acceptance of Montefort and its heritage is akin to Lois Farquar's discovery of the reality of Danielstown in *The Last September*.

Rather ironically, through the dissolute Vesta Jane meets the man who may prove to be a real lover. Unable to meet the son of an acquaintance who is flying in from Colorado, Vesta sends Jane with her chauffeur to Shannon to meet him. He proves a tall, handsome young man, and, as they confront each other, "They no sooner looked but they loved" (224). Out of context, this sudden love may appear as unduly sentimental, even for a highly poetic novel. Coming as it does, however, in a novel troubled by subjectivism, it serves as a judgment on the willingness of one who has demonstrated her capacity to distinguish reality and fantasy to avail herself of the creative "chance" of life.

Antonia's initial response to Guy's resurrection through the letters verges on the pantheistic. She feels the old force of Guy upon her emanating from the darkness of the night: "She was met at once like a wind-like rushing toward her out of the dark—her youth and Guy's from every direction. . . . All round Montefort there was going forward an entering back again into possession: the two, now one again, were again here . . ." (113). Antonia feels as if "Doom was lifted from her" and that "time again was into the clutch of herself and Guy" (113–14). Her near mystical experience is like the final intensity of light, the orgasmic sputter, before the bulb dims.

But, in the dawn of the day after, Antonia is confronted by too much evidence that the static Montefort world she has expended her energy and effort to sustain is breaking up, and that, far from living in a timeless world, the years have taken their toll of her. Lilia and Fred seem bound now to have at this late date, if not love, a relationship truly their own. Lilia's admission of Guy's other woman and her refusal to accept the packet of letters in effect earn her release from the past. Jane's entry into the Latterly world, if only as a passing observer, informs Antonia that the girl is moving beyond her grasp and into a life of her own. Angered over Jane's first contact with the castle, Antonia is mild and interested as Jane departs into Vesta's sphere again at the close.

It is Maud, however, who administers, unintentionally, the final blows to Antonia's hardened mold. Like an emerging spirit, she comes spouting forth "maledictions" from the Psalms. When Maud expresses her views about her father's role, or about what his role should be in the family, Antonia must confess, "Maud as a character had to be re-assessed . . ." (166). Antonia, like Jane before her, is forced to assess her conduct from the cold light of Maud's viewpoint, and the experience is discomfiting: Antonia flees her own bedroom, leaving "the field to Maud" (171). Maud's final impact results from her devotion to Big Ben, whose confirmation of nine o'clock on the radio she eagerly awaits each evening. Sitting in the dining room hearing "passionless Big Ben," Antonia flinches before "The sound of time, inexorably coming as it did, at once . . . absolute and fatal" (193). At the same time Jane, studying her aunt, thinks: "And I shall never see Antonia again. . . . Something has happened. Somehow she's gone,—She's old" (194).

Throughout, the narrator indirectly comments on Guy through Maud's imaginary companion, Gay David. Quite like the living members of her family, Gay is subjected to rough handling from Maud. And, if Guy's contemporaries have given him debilitating obeisance, Gay receives an unceasing flow of punches and kicks. Maud's most obvious predecessor in the novels is Theodora Thirdman of *Friends and Relations*. The narrator, along with Antonia, may well ask of Maud, "what might the future not have to fear from her?" But in a world where the temptation to effortless ennui is so great, such people are shown to be valuable.

A World of Love may be the author's covert criticism of Ireland with Guy representing the debilitating hold of the Irish past on the present and the impressionistic dreamlike style parodying the sense of unreality disarming everyday life. Whether the novel is related specifically to Ireland or not, it is a cautionary tale. The need to open windows of closed entities to the fresh air of actuality is recurringly necessary. The concluding sentence is richly ambiguous in the best Bowen manner—"They no sooner looked but they loved"—since love is both the great reality and the potent illusion.

The Little Girls

The Little Girls is Elizabeth Bowen's most intricate and subtle novel: intricate in the relationship of its components and subtle in its psychology. Allusiveness is carried to a tantalizing edge where one more step would plunge everything into an incomprehensible state. Yet the surface almost belies this allusiveness; the author has never sustained sprightlier pacing or more rapid dialogue. This engaging surface and a clever unfolding of character psychology save this novel from the fate of *A World of Love*. Though lacking in the power of her best work, *The Little Girls* is among the most impressive of Bowen's novels.

Initially asking what the consequences might be if a person rekindled relationships that have been dormant for fifty years, the novel provides one highly imaginative answer. Dinah Delacroix, still an attractive, active woman at sixty-one, decides to contact the two women with whom she was most intimate when they were all eleven and in their last term together at Saint Agatha's in the summer of 1914. By the end of part 1, Dinah (known as Dicey) has entertained at her country home Clare Burkin-Jones (Mumbo), divorcée and successful businesswoman, and Sheila Artworth (Sheikie), wife of a man whose family has long been prominent in Southstone, home of the now-vanished Saint Agatha's.

Part 2 moves back in time to deal with the closing weeks spent together by the threesome at school. The central activity follows the girls' decision to bury secretly in the school garden a coffer containing a note written in blood in a private code and various objects including a contribution by each girl known only to herself. Not until late in the novel is the nature of these contributions revealed. The section culminates with a term-end picnic and farewells, which endure until Dinah's notices in the personal columns of the *Times* and other English papers effect the reunion.

The action of part 3 follows from that of the opening sequence; Dinah talks her reluctant partners into digging up the coffer even though, as Sheila is in a position to point out, it now lies in the garden of a private home. The coffer is found empty, a discovery upsetting to Dinah. And more surprising is the collapse Dinah suffers two weeks later after being scolded by sturdy, no-nonsense Clare. The closing portion of the book revolves about the bed in which Dinah is prostrate. Sheila is on hand and in command of Dinah's two married sons; her handsome widower neighbor, Major Frank Wilkins; her youthful Maltese houseboy, Francis; and the now hangdog and troubled Clare.

Even this bare outline should reveal how the novel appears to shift in intent at the opening of the coffer. Seeming concern for the retrieval of both chest and friendship is displaced by the psychological mystery of Dinah's behavior and, retroactively, by the motivation underlying the apparent spontaneity of her decision to contact the past. The shift is, of course, seeming rather than real. Basically, the book is constructed on a cunning switch. Of the three women, Dinah appears to be the only one living a satisfying life. Why Clare and Sheila are reluctant to expose themselves to a woman whose advertisements bespeak an adventurousness they no longer possess is understandable. Yet events lead to a reversal in which Dinah emerges as the most troubled of the trio. Only gradually do we come to fathom, as Clare most evidently does, Dinah's problem and to comprehend what she means when she puzzles the others by saying such things as, "Can't you see what's happened? This us three. This going back, I mean. This began as a game, *began* as a game. Now—you see?—it's got me!"[3] The reader can take some consolation initially that neither Clare nor Sheila "sees" either.

Dinah, it becomes apparent, has had an easy life, and she has become, as Clare points out to her, "in many ways very wonderful." But, in summoning her old friends, she has encountered fears and doubts about the reality of her existence and the quality of its feeling. Though it is not crucial, it is not clear whether Dinah's doubts rose before or following the re-encounter. Dinah says, though after the fact, that she recalled her friends for hundreds of reasons (all of the facts of her life?), but Clare believes Dinah "chanced, not chose, to want Sheila and herself again" (276).

Quite appropriately, Dinah's crisis invokes for her memories of *Macbeth* and unstated echoes of life's "signifying nothing." The whole affair of the coffer suddenly becomes a symbolic testing ground for her. When illumination finally comes to Clare, she says, over the slumbering body of Dinah, "There being nothing was what you were frightened of all the time, eh? Yes. Yes, it was terrible looking down into that empty box" (277). And Frank reported earlier that, when he and Francis had lifted the distraught woman into bed, she had cried, "It's all gone, was it ever there? No, never there. Nothing. No, no, no . . ." (258). Again it is not really clear whether Dinah is referring to her own life or to life in general, but from her point of view, the distinction hardly matters.

The first indication that Dinah is cracking occurs when the women return for drinks after their digging expedition to Artworths. Having hardly arrived, Dinah announces that she must leave. When Sheila tells her that her home "won't run away," Dinah answers, "That's what it *has* done. . . . Everything has. *Now* it has, you see. Nothing's real any more . . ." (188). We may recollect with interest that, upon her introduction, Dinah is characterized as "a woman, intent on what she was doing to the point of trance . . ." (3). If, in the first stage of her awakening, Dinah must question the nature of her own reality, in the second stage, her personal being is called to an accounting. Taking umbrage at one of Dinah's remarks, Clare gives her an objective characterization of herself; she calls Dinah "Circe" and "a cheat. A player-about. Never once have you played fair, all along the line"; then she adds, "Some of us more than *think* we feel" (230).

This announcement amplifies earlier statements Clare and Sheila have made about Dinah. When Dinah's notices first came to their attention, and Clare and Sheila met to decide whether or not to answer her, they most readily recall Dinah as "too self-centered" (40). Throughout the book they refer to her as "Young Lochinvar" and "Ba-lamb." And, after seeing the present-day Dinah, Sheila can still say she has "never yet outgrown being a selfish child" (201). When she becomes quite worked up over Dinah, she says, "What makes me so mad is the way things are showered on to her that she hasn't the sense to value or understand. Showered" (201). Moreover, the whole world built about Dinah attests to its unreality and its accommodation of her. Francis, with his Walter Mitty–like projections of secret-service adventure, is a fitting occupant of a demi-paradise in which his mistress has at her beck and call a handsome gentleman who helps her with tending a garden where innocence clearly prevails. The grotto with its fanciful collection of mementos pried loose from people, though they are items "which they couldn't have normally borne to part with," and a place destined to confound future people is the perfect activity for an individual who enjoys, even if she does not comprehend, life.

In addition to the other names she calls Dinah, Clare claims she is an "enchantress's child," and this term provides a clue for a reading of the wonderfully realized 1914 scenes. Dinah and her mother, Mrs. Piggott (pig it?),[4] live in the cozy little Feverel Cottage (can we doubt the author's intent that we remember the raising of Richard in George Meredith's *The Ordeal of Richard Feverel*?). Here, supported by a wealthy cousin, Mrs. Piggott indulges her two loves, fine china and books (later there is repeated reference to the books in Dinah's bedroom); here, "Mrs. Piggott and [Dinah] had . . . spun round themselves a tangible web, through whose transparency, layers deep, one glimpsed some fixed, perhaps haunted, other dimension" (85).

Though there are passing references to the visits of Major Birkin-Jones to Feverel Cottage, it is not until the end of part 2 that it is possible to comprehend his love for Dinah's mother. On the verge of reporting for active duty, for war is imminent, he appears at the picnic late to say farewell to Mrs. Piggott. She has been willing to take, if not to give; when she folds her arms and presses "them against herself" he says, "You're cold" (151). Later it is disclosed that Dinah's father threw himself under a train before her birth, and, although no explanation for his action is proffered, none seems needed. When Mrs. Piggott is sick in bed, Dinah wishes to quote a line from *Macbeth* and chooses, suggestively, "Was my father a traitor, mother?" (244). This question implies her recognition of what the loss of a father may have cost her life.

Technically, the novel's middle section is a tour de force in maintaining our attention on the surface action and implanting hints about Major Birkin-Jones in such a way that the disclosure of his love comes at once as surprise to us—and all the more so for having taken place under our very eyes.

Dinah's illness proves double-edged. For her it is purgative; for her circle of acquaintances it is rejuvenative. Frank is stunned. A selfish man himself, as Sheila observes, it is ironic that he is not aware that Dinah has fobbed him off, literally and figuratively, with a mask. But he does come to bury his head in her pillow. Sheila, hitherto somewhat ineffectual, finds a true outlet for her desire to be useful. Tending Dinah gives her an opportunity to repay her one-time exit from the deathroom of her lover, which has haunted her. By way of reward, she inherits, as it were in Dinah's offspring, the sons she has longed to have. For her part, Clare realizes how she has permitted business to dehumanize her and deny the feelings of others, for, standing over the prostrate Dinah, she says to herself: "I did not comfort you. Never have I comforted you. Forgive me" (277).

Clare's final admission of responsibility toward others is analogous with the change Dinah experiences. Fittingly, the book ends with Dinah waking from a long sleep. The brief exchange between herself and Clare reveals, for all its terseness, that Dinah has shed her childlike attitude to life, along with her terrifying sense of meaninglessness, and has assumed her proper role in the present. Upon awakening Dinah queries: "Who's there?" "Mumbo." "Not Mumbo. Clare. Clare, where have you been?" (277). It is a paradox worthy of life that the innocence that came to trouble Dinah is the kind that made possible not only her own salvation but also the resurrection of her closest friends. This paradox recurs consistently in the author's fiction.

When we at last learn what items the girls placed in the coffer, it can be seen that each buried something really requisite to her life. If not in actuality, then metaphysically, events allow the women to repossess what was secretly hidden. Dinah's contribution was a gun, symbol of violence, without which, according to other Bowen novels, life is incomplete. The results of violence, if not the act itself, appear in the novel in the form of the bruise on Dinah's forehead, discovered when she is found by Francis slumped over. And, along with the late disclosure of Mr. Piggott's violent death, come several hints of contemplated suicide on Dinah's part.

Clare buried a copy of Shelley's poetry, believing herself through with it. Her failed marriage and her protective brittleness readily enough indicate her loss of a sense of poetry in life and her indifference to the humanitarianism Shelley advocated. Not so readily translatable as the gun and the book is Sheila's contribution to the casket of an extra toe she has had removed. But, when she mentions how embarrassed she was over the toe, it may be surmised that, in being unwilling to accept her fate or situation, her unwillingness to acknowledge the sliver of flesh has remained as her inability to accept the events of her life, one that accounts for her tensions and hypersensitivity.

Eva Trout

A World of Love and *The Little Girls* seek to justify the image of hope and promise that survive the Holocaust of *The Heat of the Day.* Both novels find rehabilitation possible in the modern world, but Elizabeth Bowen's tenth novel, *Eva Trout or Changing Scenes*, discloses that the scene has indeed changed; the honeymoon is over. The world of *Eva Trout* is askew and romantically bloated; it is studded with heavy operatic names like Iseult, Eric, and Constantine. Fittingly a heroine with the sturdy, fundamental name of Eva Trout desires normalcy, but she, as the novel implies, is asking too much of our times. Long denied a sane, stable existence, Eva, on the verge of reaping her desires and of achieving respectable communication with the world, is struck down in a melodramatically bizarre and ludicrously contrived manner. *Eva Trout* is Bowen's contribution to the black humor of the 1960s. What makes this report tolerable is, typically enough with Bowen, the romping delight of the narrative voice that delights in the inexhaustibleness of the human condition, whatever its manifestations.

Mrs. Iseult Arbles, on her way to visit Eva, pauses in Broadstairs to visit the Charles Dickens's room in Bleak House. This room gives the narrator an opportunity to observe, "It took Dickens not to be eclipsed by Eva."[5] Eva, a "she-Cossack," is the largest of the author's heroines, both literally and figuratively. But she shares with her predecessors an abnormal rearing that renders her conduct of relationships highly unnatural. A combination of miseducation or noneducation has made Eva a conversational misfit; as a result, drama follows from her encounters with communication. When is Eva to be believed, and to what extent? Conversely, how will she interpret or misinterpret the signals she receives from the abnormal or nervous human beings surrounding her? A trout out of water in a neurotic world, Eva wants a husband and a child. But how to acquire them?

The book begins when Eva is boarding with Eric and Iseult Arbles who live on a fruit farm in Worcestershire. She is almost twenty-four, and when she has her birthday she is to come into a fortune. Chiefly she occupies herself with the local rectory children of Mr. and Mrs. Dancey. Her favorite is Henry, twelve, perhaps because "she [can] not boss him and he [can] mortify her . . ." (15). Quite evidently Eva is bored with her situation; and, like Bowen heroines before her, she is eager to begin her own life. The principal action of part 1 involves Eva's sudden and secretive departure for the Broadstairs area where she purchases a large furnished home near the sea. Life, presumably, begins with a home, preferably an older one that boasts a past bespeaking settlement. When she becomes wealthy, Eva fills this home with the latest in electrical equipment. The electric typewriter, stereo, movie projector, tape recorder, and computer (on order) are to place her abreast of her time and, perhaps, represent a reflexive determination to modernize her capacity to communicate.

After the house is to come what is more readily purchasable by Eva than a husband—a child. But Eva's nature does not permit her simply to fly to the United States where she intends to make this transaction; she must prepare the way. During a visit with Eva, Iseult proposes that Eva spend Christmas with the Arbles. Eva refuses on the grounds that she will, at that time, be having a baby. Unhindered by Eva, Iseult, realizing a time lapse of nine months between an earlier visit to Eva by Eric at Christmas, assumes the obvious.

Eva's announcement is her way of settling a grudge held against Iseult that dates from the days when Iseult was Miss Smith, teacher in a private girls' school, and Eva was one of her pupils. Eva arrived at the school after she had wearied of trailing about the world with her father and his male lover, Constantine, and had insisted that she be allowed to settle into a more natural life. Having passed through the hands of a series of indifferent governesses who served in place of her mother long since killed in a plane crash, Eva is elated to be recognized as existing by Miss Smith, and she experiences the first passion of her life: "Till Iseult came, no human being had ever turned upon Eva their full attention—an attention which could seem to be love. Eva knew nothing of love but that it existed—that, she should know, having looked on at it. *Her* existence had gone by under a shadow: the shadow of Willy Trout's total attachment to Constantine" (18). Like other Bowen characters who are charged with reciprocating the idealistic demands of other Bowen heroines, Iseult hedges in her response, and Eva construes her caution as rejection. So the seed of antipathy comes to be planted.

When, a few years later, Willy Trout commits suicide and Constantine assumes the role of guardian, Eva decides she would like to board with the intellectual Iseult and her workingman husband on their fruit farm. The Arbles welcome Eva—but for financial reasons. Like Portia in *The Death of the Heart*, Eva enters a household where marriage is proving less than satisfactory: "the marriage was founded on a cerebral young woman's first physical passion" (19). Eric is disappointed because there are no children; Iseult, already chaffing at a restrictive life with a failed fruit farmer cum garage man, is troubled by his declining interest in her. Eric's eventual interest in Eva is not calculated to ease matters at all. Eva's pregnancy gambit proves to be the coup de grace to the marriage.

Not until eight years later does Eva learn that the Arble marriage failed to survive her implied relationship with Eric. However, this novel, and others by the author, shares an ambivalence toward violence wrought by the subjective innocent. There is no hint of loss, no sense of real pain over the Arbles' separation. Upon her return to England, Eva begins to pick up the ends of her earlier life. She finds Eric living contentedly with a common-law wife who has borne him two children. Iseult is located on the Continent but is easily enough lured back into Eva's orbit. Before long Iseult and Eric are back together again, and this time, seemingly, they are truly in love. No mention is made of the two children and their mother. Such is the modern world.

The baby boy Eva acquires surreptitiously in Chicago and christens Jeremy proves to be a deaf-mute, and, in the years of Eva's absence from England, she has lived in a series of American cities in an effort to find help for her son. When he is eight, she decides the time has come for them to return to her country and to locate, though such is never stated directly, a father for Jeremy. They settle in a London hotel, and, after Jeremy is set to sculpting with a private tutor, Eva leaves for Cambridge to seek Henry Dancey who is now a student.

The final sequence of absurdity has its beginning when Iseult, back from London, "borrows" Jeremy from his sculpting instructress in order to have a visit with him since she still assumes he has been fathered by Eric. When Jeremy fails to return to his mother at the hotel, she becomes distraught; her mind leaps immediately to the probability of kidnapping. Before she does anything drastic, however, Jeremy wanders in. He, of course, cannot explain matters to her. Unnerved, Eva decides to quit London for a time, and, leaving all of their possessions at the hotel, she and Jeremy make for Fontainebleau. While here, she fortuitously becomes acquainted with a doctor and his wife who have been working with deaf-mutes with considerable success. The couple agrees to accept Jeremy as long as he can live with them and Eva will absent herself. When Eva returns to England and Henry, she proposes marriage to the young man, who really is quite fond of her. He refuses. Then, as usual with Eva, who prefers to have the appearance of propriety if not the reality of it for the benefit of the Arbles and Constantine, she asks him to depart with her from Victoria Station as if he were going to marry her, and he agrees to her request.

Thus, the culminating scene takes place at Victoria. And indeed Iseult, Eric, and Constantine are on hand in a festive mood—as is Jeremy, who has been brought from France for the occasion. Before coming to the station, however, he has visited his old hotel to pick up some things left behind. He is delighted and surprised to find among the Trout goods a pistol, a real one, though he is not aware that it is. Bowen has earlier shown how the gun became so located. It belongs to Eric but turned up among Iseult's possessions when she went to the Continent. She has decided to bring it back to England in order to return it to him. Not wishing to carry the gun about with her, she is inspired, when she becomes aware of Eva's stored possessions in London, to deposit the gun temporarily with these.

There are two moments of drama at Victoria. First, Henry tells Eva that he has changed his mind; he really wishes to marry her. Second, Jeremy, rushing forward to greet his mother, playfully points the gun at her, pulls the trigger, and the gun fires. Eva drops to the pavement dead, and the novel ends. Though the book invokes a Dickensian world as a context for Eva, it more fittingly reminds one of Thomas Hardy and of *Jude the Obscure* in particular. Eva, like Jude, has aspirations that both her limited awareness and her incessant misfortune abrogate.

The novel is very entertaining; Bowen is too much the professional for *Eva Trout* to be otherwise. But in retrospect, we wonder if it adds up to much. A residue of dissatisfaction seems almost inevitable. The author's work gives a sense of the untidiness and unpredictability of life, and her books realize her own insistence that major characters retain the capacity to unfold throughout a narrative. *Eva Trout*, conversely, is held too tightly in thrall by its basic narrative diagram. Eva, child of violence and seeker of a normal life, reverses the usual sequence of husband, child, house, and, when she is on the verge of attaining the husband, she comes full circle to her true inheritance of violence.

Eva Trout, in one sense an un–Bowen–like work, appears to be a send up of many of the author's recurring interests and fictional elements. This may account for the critical reservations it has prompted. Certainly it is a work asking to be read in its own grotesque terms as the numerous references to Dickens seemingly encourage. At bottom is the great Bowen theme of insecurity, and *Eva Trout* is either the final exorcising of a recurring nightmare or a bold attempt to laugh it out of court. Eva's lifelong handicapped pursuit of identity is by turns noble, ludicrous, and pathetic. As well, given the dislocations of the times, it is doomed. The fact remains that all human beings, even if fish out of water, must make their lives—if they are to live—by fashioning themselves. Elizabeth Bowen's last response to this, as *Eva Trout* demonstrates, is to somehow simultaneously laugh and cry.

Chapter Five

The Shorter Fiction

Elizabeth Bowen clearly enjoyed working back and forth between novels and shorter works. She has implied that the two forms may reflect alternate selves. Noting the amount of fantasy in her stories, something she eschews in her novels, she says,

> If I were a short story writer only, I might well seem to be out of balance. But recall, more than half of my life is under the steadying influence of the novel, with its calmer, stricter, more orthodox demands: into the novel goes such taste as I have for rational behaviour and social portraiture. The short story, as *I* see it to be, allows for what is crazy about humanity: obstinacies, inordinate heroisms, "immortal longings."[1]

The Writings of Stories

Bowen wrote her first story, "Breakfast," when she was twenty. This work and those that followed in the next two years did not find a publisher. A break occurred when Olive Willis, her headmistress when she was at Downe House, introduced her to the noted writer Rose Macaulay. This contact led to her first appearance in print, in *The Saturday Westminster.* In 1923, the same year as her marriage, her first story collection, *Encounters*, appeared. Between 1926 and 1945 five additional collections were published, more or less alternating with her novels. In 1959 Alfred A. Knopf in New York published her own selection of her best eighteen stories in *Stories by Elizabeth Bowen*, and six years later Jonathan Cape in London published another of her personal selections, *A Day in the Dark and Other Stories*. This collection contains twenty stories, four of them appearing in book form for the first time. The two selections have eleven stories in common and presumably are the works by which the author primarily wishes to be represented.

Perhaps the first observation to make about these particular eleven stories is that they include Bowen's five longest or, in effect, her five novellas: "The Disinherited," "A Love Story," "A Summer Night," "The Happy Autumn Fields," and, the longest, "Ivy Gripped the Steps." The length of these stories, in a publishing sense, has complicated her general exposure as a story writer.

First, by including these five works both of her personal selections limited the choice of other material; second, her appearance in short story anthologies, where space is at a premium, has precluded the inclusion of one or another of her novellas, though arguably they can be regarded as the best and most representative of her work, including the novels. Two of the eleven stories are often anthologized, "The Demon Lover," and "Her Table Spread." The remaining titles in this selected group are, "Look at All Those Roses," "No. 16," "Reduced," and "Mysterious Kôr." My selection of stories to discuss in this chapter indicates that I have not agreed entirely with Bowen's own choices.

That situations and character types recur in Bowen's more than eighty stories is to be expected, but what surprises is the accomplished variety. The single largest grouping concerns children and adolescents being prematurely or sharply exposed to painful circumstances, which indicates the rich fictional resources of the author's own early years. There are a considerable number of ghost stories and related to these another group involving disturbed civilians reacting to the incessant bombing of London during World War II. In another grouping Bowen offers her versions of established story types. For example, "Look at All Those Roses" is the familiar formula of the motoring couple experiencing a breakdown in an isolated area where the lone nearby dwelling is inhabited by unusual individuals. "A Love Story" juxtaposes several sets of interacting couples one evening at an Irish coastal hotel. "The Cheery Soul" tells of an invited guest arriving at a home for a holiday visit and being involved in totally unforeseen circumstances.

In the Preface to *Stories by Elizabeth Bowen* the author offers several insights into her approach to the short story. Stories, of course, displaying a concentration of effect impossible in a novel and revolving around a single crisis, aim at a "central, single effect."[2] Place and mood are crucial in her stories, and she admits that "On the whole, places more often than faces have sparked off stories." The creative imagination does not conform to a formula, though Bowen's comments suggest a representative process. An observed or imagined scene provokes a sense of a dramatic situation that calls forth a particular character, "*the* one" on whom the crisis will "act most strongly." She sees the writer as fundamentally an explorer: "It could seem to me that stories, with their *dramatis personae*, pre-exist, only wait to be come upon! I know I do not invent them; I discover them. Though that does not mean that they are easily told. On me devolves the onus of narration." This in turn confirms the creative fact "that every short story is an experiment."

A strong sense of place and mood characterizes these stories. The manner of telling is impressionistic because the style aims to suggest indirectly the psychological and emotional states of the principal characters. Very often a story will move back and forth in time between a determinant past and a resultant present. Dialogue usually generates most of its significance between the lines. Stories often end with what the author calls "a query," which leaves the reader conjecturing about what has actually taken place or is likely to ensue.

In this chapter I consider a dozen or so of Bowen's finest stories. The four groupings provide a fair indication of her most pervasive and successful basic situations, narrative setups, and manner of retailing. The inclusion of a story under one heading does not preclude its relationship with material found under a different one. The first group of stories, for example, shows a particular emphasis on the potency of locale, but this characteristic is evident, if less centrally, in virtually all of the stories.

Haunted Houses

For Elizabeth Bowen, houses are powerful presences. Important in most of her novels, they are, if anything, even more enmeshed in character psyches in the stories. Some of the houses are "haunted" by presences that prey upon susceptible imaginations and so feed fears. This openness to haunting is one way the author exposes the resourcelessness of seemingly sophisticated moderns. For all their apparent awareness, these exemplars of the unexamined life inhabit surfaces that can be cracked and exposed. The reaction to this becomes the focal point of these stories.

"The Cat Jumps." The Harold Wrights have bought the country home Rose Hill, vacant for the two years since the former owner, Harold Bentley, cut his wife into pieces and deposited them in various parts of the house. The bright, advanced-thinking Wrights with their "shadowless, thoroughly disinfected minds" are not to be put off like others by the grotesque associations.[3] In fact, exploiting the situation, Wrights gets a knockdown bargain. The occasion of the story is the Wrights's first weekend party at Rose Hill. It proves unsuccessful. The weather is oppressively overcast and damp. One of the guests, the single Muriel, is preoccupied by the sensational Bentley case and insists on sharing her knowledge of the gruesome facts. Tension mounts and tempers fray. As the second evening falls, "You would have said that each personality had been attacked by some kind of decomposition" (281). "Sex antagonism" surfaces as the women reveal their vestigal fear of male aggression, and all of the males begin to look like Harold Bentley. Told with sly wit, the story builds stroke by stroke its growing sense of alarm. The narrator, all coolness, concludes by describing the final sequence of action triggered by Muriel and the reactions that follow. The Wrights are not alone in this blanket exposure.

"Foothold." While similar, "The Cat Jumps" and "Foothold" offer a revealing contrast. Behind this story are both D. H. Lawrence and Henry James. Gerard and Janet's move into a large country home appears to have changed Janet. In reporting this to their bachelor visitor Thomas, Gerard wonders if they should move again. The question is, has Janet discovered or invented the ghost Clara? Gerard jokes about Clara when Janet is present, but to Thomas he confides, "She's seeing too much of this ghost," adding, "She wouldn't if things were all right with her."[4] These two effete males, at the extreme from the passionate Harold Bentley, cannot comprehend the problem of this physically unfulfilled woman. Gerard is driven to ask Thomas, who is beginning to write a study of monasteries, what he thinks Janet's true feelings are. Janet is, in fact, one of those mind-oriented women that Lawrence so loathed: her "bodily attraction . . . modified by the domination of her clear fastidious aloof mind over her body." What is disturbing about Janet's situation is that she is "civilized too deep down." From the start Janet and the house are linked. Her increasing awareness of its size has led her to the Jamesian sense of an alternate life. She tells Thomas, "there's more room every day. I suppose it must be underneath." These attenuated beings have, in effect, sacrificed their vital selves to materialism. As they sit and talk, their principal activity, while "sinking a little deeper into the big chairs," Thomas exclaims, "Would we really ever have known each other before there was this kind of chair? I've a theory that absolute comfort runs round the circle to the same point as asceticism." Janet's insulated boredom has allowed Clara to gain a foothold. Ironically Clara attests to something remaining vital within Janet though she is a damning comment on the males. Thomas has some insight into this and sufficient pride to feel embarrassment for Gerard and himself: "how much less humiliating for them both it would have been if she'd taken a lover."

"The Demon Lover." Elizabeth Bowen's best-known story, "The Demon Lover," is certainly her most controversial. This ghost story, superbly evoking place and mood, charts the protagonist's developing hysteria, and relentlessly sustains tension until the shattering denouement.

Like many Londoners, Mrs. Kathleen Drover and her family have been forced to leave the city because of the bombing, which has weakened the structure of their home. On the day of the story Mrs. Drover is in London to do a number of errands. The last of these, late in the day, is collecting some wanted articles from the closed-up house. The imagery indicates the link between the house and her subconscious. If it is haunted it is because she is. The letter on the hall table reflects the long suppressed irrational terror that her long-dead fiancé will keep his parting threat to return and claim her.

Does the letter literally exist? The story teasingly leaves open the possibility: the fiancé "was reported missing, and presumed killed" and, as the famous story of Robert Graves attests, soldiers did return from "the dead" (222). If the letter is authentic then Mrs. Drover is part of an amazing story of a lover's patience and is truly in the hands of a clever madman. So far as a reading of the tale is concerned it hardly matters: to Mrs. Drover it is real and her fear-driven energy gains a willing suspension of disbelief. However, the subtle undertext provides a psychological explanation.

Mrs. Drover, already dislocated by the bombing and the forced move, weary at the end of the day, depressed by the ambience of her street and the interior of her house, is vulnerable to attack. A naturally fearful person, she normally keeps her fears willfully under control with the aid of a safe family context. Now she undergoes a Lawrencean experience in which the suppressed is loosed to rise up and strike. "Ink dark" clouds pile up as Mrs. Drover approaches her house, and the rain comes "crashing down" shortly after she enters (220). Her "once familiar street" proves "unfamiliar" and isolated since "no human eye watched." Only after difficulty with the lock does the "warped" door open, and "dead air" greets her as she enters. Inside she is "perplexed" by the darkened interior. The house, with "cracks in the structure," is not a safe place.

With Mrs. Drover in an unsettled state in a disturbing environment, it is appropriate to recall Bowen's indication that she seeks to put into situations the very characters who will be most sensitive to them. Mrs. Drover's "most normal expression was one of controlled worry, but of assent" (220). This assent indicates her preference for a peaceful environment. Furthermore, "Since the birth of the third of her little boys, attended by a quite serious illness, she had had an intermittent muscular flicker to the left of her mouth," suggesting further the pressure of her "controlled worry." The exposition reinforces this developing profile. Twenty-five years previous, in August of 1916, when she and her fiancé are parting (for what proves to be the last time), she thinks of "the moment when she could go running back . . . into the safe arms of her mother and sister, and cry: 'What shall I do, what shall I do? He has gone'" (221). (In the present, Mrs. Drover, who likes to be cared for, is wearing a jumper knitted for her by her sister.) Her family do not care for the man and later do not regret his loss. Her mother does not believe he loves her daughter though he "was set on" her. What the mother cannot appreciate is her own daughter's motivation, which also devalues love. Mrs. Drover recalls that "He was never kind" to her and recognizes, even at the time of their farewell, that his statement "I shall be with you . . . sooner or later" is "unnatural" and threatening.

His cruelty actually underlined his commitment to her and represented the security and safety that, more than love, she craved. She may also have sensed the limitations of her appeal to other men, for in the years that follow none come forward and she remains within the security of her family. At thirty-two, however, to the relief of both herself and her family, she had wed William Drover and settled into a quiet marriage. Nothing about Drover is related, but he provided all that was required for "Her movements as Mrs. Drover were circumscribed" (222).

The story is notably ambiguous about the letter writer, reflecting, apparently, Mrs. Drover's thought, since he is spoken of as "dead or living." Dead in actuality, he lives deep within her. She stops rummaging in her trunk after realizing she is "kneeling with her back exposed to the empty room." With the trunk now open she reaches a crisis: "her married London home's whole air of being a cracked cup from which memory, with its reassuring power, had either evaporated or leaked away. . . . The hollowness of the house this evening cancelled years and years of voices, habits and steps" (222). With her protective insulation torn, Mrs. Drover is open to primal fears. With the disturbances of the time, unsettling enough, being reinforced by the oppressive day, the unnatural silence, the unreality of the house, and the naturally nervous Mrs. Drover's shield of memory weakened, breakdown must follow. The very qualities that made the fiancé attractive, his possessive hardness, now make him a horror. Mrs. Drover's fears relate to those experienced by the women in "The Cat Jumps," whose terror of male violence made withdrawal and flight requisite.

Memorable Visits

Many of Elizabeth Bowen's stories begin with the protagonist arriving for a visit. Naturally, visiting and houses go together, and the visitor's first impression of a house or a neighborhood may provide a forewarning of the nature of the house's owner or may signal the consequences of the visit. Since the author builds most of her stories through exposing individuals to the unexpected, visiting is a ready means of achieving this. Some stories concern a single visit, others involve a series of them and, in this latter case, the story usually establishes a contrast in life-styles. The motif of the visit, as with that of the house, is by no means confined to the stories immediately under consideration.

"A Day in the Dark." Fifteen-year-old Barbie is apprehensive as she approaches Miss Banderry's house in a small Irish town. The house stands out from its terrace by virtue of its "sombrely painted red" door (12). "A Day in the Dark" is reminiscent of the Paris portion of *The House in Paris*. In this rare instance for Bowen of first-person narration, the older Barbie recalls the occasion and the summer it took place in the light of subsequent events. These are memories she will never forget and, perhaps, never get over. Barbie does not confront Miss Banderry unprepared. The youthful bachelor uncle on whose farm Barbie is spending the summer has an attraction–repulsion relationship with this older woman who owns the neighboring farm. Barbie is paying the visit to Miss Banderry to save him from facing her, and she feels an exultation in being able to serve. Even so, she can hardly be expected to appreciate the hold Miss Banderry has over her innately weak uncle. With him Barbie is experiencing her first and probably intensest love ever: it was "a summer like no other and which could never be again" (17). Naturally it is a relationship of which Miss Banderry cannot approve, as the uncle's suicide after Barbie's departure at summer's end makes clear.

Miss Banderry is a proud and willful woman who scorns men or at least those who are unmanly. It is not clear whether she thinks she should have been a man or resents that women must defer to men. At one time the Banderrys were a prospering milling family in Moher, but because of her "hopeless brother" the business was sold. In her opinion such would never have happened had she been in charge. From her brother she demanded her share of the sale, and when after this he cannot pay his other debts he hangs himself. In her conversation with Miss Banderry, who refers to her uncle repeatedly as "my lord," Barbie notes, "Her amorous hostility to my uncle . . . unsheathed itself when she likened him to the brother she drove to death" (17). "A Day in the Dark" is notable for its remarkable compactness and suggestive obliqueness and is consummate in handling the conversation between the younger and older women. From the opening evocation of Miss Banderry's terrace until the close the tension never eases.

"No. 16." Jane Oates, thirty and never touched by a man, is delighted by her invitation to visit Maxmilian Bewdons in "No. 16." She has written to him after he gave her first novel a glowing review in a second-rate paper. The provincial and unsophisticated Jane is unaware that Bewdons is a literary has-been; she is dumbfounded when she arrives at Medussa Terrace, St. John's Wood, for the terrace is awaiting the wreckers: doors and windows are boarded up, and stucco walls are crumbling. Only No. 16, "tacked, living, to the hulk of the terrace," is still inhabited (229). This is a story about sickness, literal and figurative. Ironically, this luncheon should not be taking place. Though ill with the flu, Jane does not want to miss this opportunity. She leaves her south London room early in order to have time to find her way. Consequently she misses Mrs. Bewdon's telegram telling her not to come because her husband has the flu. Jane has arranged for him to read her unpublished poetry. Bewdons is caught up in a sense of life's drive toward destruction—of buildings, reputations, and bodies. Out of a sense of the purity of art and the futility of fame he tells her to burn her poems. Because he touches her face and holds her hands his words carry emotional force, and so, returning to her room, Jane climbs back into bed where "Her pillow sounded hollow with notes and knockings, notes and knockings you hear in condemned rooms" (235). It is imagery that does not augur well for the future of Jane's fragile creative forces.

"Ivy Gripped the Steps." Barbie in "A Day in the Dark" and Jane in "No. 16" pay single visits to unhappy and warped individuals. While the experience of the child Gavin Doddington in "Ivy Gripped the Steps" is different and seemingly fortuitous, the results are conclusively more devastating. This is the story of destructiveness resulting from youthful expectations being blighted. Published in *Horizon* in 1945, it remarkably anticipates L. P. Hartley's 1953 novel *The Go-Between*, in which Leo Colston, in his sixties, looks back to the summer of 1900 when he was twelve and visited a country estate. So traumatic were the events of this holiday they destroyed his capacity for love and society. His recollection is paradoxical, for the zenith of his life, his time, as he saw it then, among the gods and goddesses was what destroyed him emotionally.

In "Ivy Gripped the Steps" the aging Doddington comes to Southstone where as a child he experienced what proved the greatest joy of his life and, in a spiritual sense, its end. World War II is drawing to a close and the once-fashionable seaside resort, after years of army occupation and of being in the front lines, appears seedy. It is the image of Doddington's inner being. Drawn again to the former home of the handsome Lilian Nicholson in what was "one of the best residential avenues," he finds decay (288).

Frail child of a struggling gentleman farmer, Gavin, is invited, ironically, for the sake of his health, to the seaside home of the newly widowed Lilian because she and his mother were the closest of friends at school. Lilian's fashionable life is a revelation to the eight-year-old. The visits recur, and Gavin, in his own way, falls in love with Lilian, who in turn acquiesces in his intense uncomprehended feelings. Lilian is not malign, but simply thoughtless, and such words as "tentative" and "vague" properly attach to her. Involved in a game whose impact on Gavin she fails to register, she says to him, "Why do I stay here; what am I doing? Why don't we go right away somewhere, Gavin; you and I." Her social group is uneasy over her relationship with the boy, but only Admiral Concannon challenges her conduct. In seeking to flirt with him as well, she has picked the wrong man, and he minces no words:

> "Flirtation's always been off my beat. . . . If you can't live without it, you cannot, and that is that. If you have to be dangled after, you no doubt will be. But don't, my dear girl, go for that to the wrong shop. It would have been enough, where I am concerned, to watch you making a ninnie of that unfortunate boy."
>
> "Who, poor funny little Gavin?" said Mrs. Nicholson. "Must I have nothing?—I have no little dog. You would not like it, even, if I had a real little dog" (315).

This is what Gavin inadvertently overhears. He is crushed, and despair "gripped him and gripped his limbs." The word echoes in the present as he studies her deserted house infested with ivy, "The process of strangulation" palpable. Shortly after his shock Lilian dies, and Gavin is "frozen."

The leisurely pace of the story, Bowen's longest, conveys how naturally and how inevitably the ingredients of disaster accumulate. The brief scenes of Gavin's harsher home life clarify his deep response to Lilian's silken net. With her, as he says, as nowhere else, he "comes alive." Pathos marks the conclusion. Doddington cannot resist revisiting the house once occupied by Concannon and currently occupied by an army unit. As he stands looking at it a uniformed woman comes down the steps whom he seeks to engage in conversation. As he tells her, "I've got nobody to talk to. . . ." When he lights a cigarette in the falling dusk she sees "the face of someone dead" and registers "a whole stopped mechanism for feeling." Earlier involved with a woman too old for him, he now confronts one too young. The concluding sentence, her question to him, is positively Hardyesque, "Why don't you pick on some place where you know someone?" (320).

"The Queer Heart." The three previous "visiting" stories focus on the visitor and his or her experience. In "The Queer Heart" the emphasis is on the one visited. Mrs. Cadman is undergoing one of her unmarried sister Rosa's semi-annual visits. Mrs. Cadman is easy-going and self-indulgent. Not so Rosa, and when Mr. Cadman was alive she was not welcome. Mrs. Cadman does not enjoy Rosa's stays because then her daughter Lucille who lives with her joins with Rosa to criticize her conduct and appearance. This mother–daughter relationship exists in reverse, for Mrs. Cadman has a face "as ingenuous as a little girl's," is piggish with sweets, and perpetually bangs doors. Rosa's current stay is unique, first, because she becomes seriously ill, and, second, because what she recalls from her past validates Mrs. Cadman's worth whatever her foibles. Mrs. Cadman dutifully sits at Rosa's bedside though disliking her sister's uncongenial bitterness. She tells Mrs. Cadman when and why she first assumed her stance toward life. One Christmas, when they were very young, Mrs. Cadman asked for and received a doll Rosa had also wanted. The child Rosa found her own way of responding: "I could have fretted, seeing you take everything. One thing, then another. But I was shown. God taught me to pity you."[5] Mrs. Cadman's response is understandable, "I didn't *mean* any harm—why, I was quite a little thing. I don't even remember." She reminds her sister that her life has had its "ups and downs" and "hasn't been all jam," but essentially she is moved to tenderness and, thinking of Rosa's "poor queer heart," she thinks, "No wonder you wanted Lucille . . . you did ought to have had that fairy doll." Rosa is unattractive in her self-righteousness, yet this is a touching and ambivalent story in its sad sense of life's unfairness. The evidence suggests that discontent and unfulfillment breed themselves as happiness does not.

Deracination

Several of Elizabeth Bowen's stories feature hollow men and women suffering modern malaise. Angst-ridden, they dally with the present and dread the future. Like a squirrel in a circular cage they endlessly tread their discontents. Many, seeing themselves as victimized by changing times and robbed of their expectations, are immobilized by the problem of finding alternate lives. Perhaps the chief casualty of the general rootlessness is love.

"The Disinherited." About change and disappointment, "The Disinherited" explores the gap between desire and possibility. A character thinks, "One is enpowered to live fully: occasion does not offer" (62). The drama turns on the quiet "modern" wife Marianne Harvey who begins unaware of the malaise of "hollow idleness" that holds in thrall her new friend Davina. The final uncertainty involves her future and that of her marriage. Davina, penniless at twenty-nine, has come to live on her aunt Mrs. Archworth near an old village: "To earn a living was out of the question: she had no idea what to do." Love affairs and other extravagances have absorbed her inheritance. Like the unhappy woman in Lawrence's "The Rocking-Horse Winner," her mind in money haunted.

Above the village is a new raw housing estate emblematically in the midst of "wiry grass that had lost its nature, being no longer meadow and not yet lawn." Here Marianne lives with her husband, Matthew, fifteen years her senior and recently retired from the Civil Service owing to ill health. He is gripped by a dread of desiccation, so it is understandable why acquaintance with Davina has "extended deliciously, painfully" Marianne's hitherto complacent consciousness. It is autumn and images of decay abound as she falls under the spell of Davina's sterile worldliness.

The central action takes place on a November night when Matthew is away in London and a group of Davina's friends are gathering for a party at Lord Thingummy's large, closed-up country house. One of her former lovers, Oliver, who ekes out a living by cataloguing the libraries of estates, is currently going through the library here. Before Davina and Marianne drive to the party, Davina borrows money from her aunt's chauffeur Prothero, payment in effect for the kisses that attest to her corruption. Feeling both attraction and repulsion for Prothero, Davina instinctively recognizes him a criminal, and, indeed, he is a murderer who has changed identities.

The party gathers together a collection of lost souls "frozen" into discontent amidst the "glacial sheeted" furniture. Oliver, "a broken-spirited Viking," is another Davina: "The old order left him stranded, the new offered him no place." Such descriptives as *empty*, *askew*, *peevish* and *tarnished* characterize these damned. Though Marianne's heart has been "set on this evening's pleasure," she quickly wishes herself "safe at home."

In "The Disinherited's" five-part structure the party scene is framed by opening and closing passages of similar length and is itself divided in the middle by a lengthy sequence devoted to Prothero. This latter has troubled some commentators. One suggests it is a "sub-Lawrentian fantasy which dilutes the story's subtlety," and is an instance "of flagrant self-indulgence."[6] Another sees the story "lumbered" by Prothero's "melodramatic history."[7] In fact, it gives Bowen's vision encompassing symmetry. If Davina and her friends are emotionally sterile, described by the imagery of ice, then Prothero is likewised fixed, although in futile passion: night after night he writes frantic letters of pleading and explanation to the woman whose love he feared to lose and has smothered, "Anita I love you Anita, Anita where are you? . . . come back . . . I won't hurt you, come back, come back come back" (50). These contrasting extremes, in which futile repetition substitutes for living, are equally corrosive.

Following the party Oliver deludes Marianne with tears and seduces her. She returns home having been infected by the malaise, but to what degree we do not know. To Matthew, newly returned from London, Marianne looks "as though it were she who were just back from a journey and could still find no place to rest." To his question about what is bothering her she replies, "Perhaps I have got a slight chill" (59). Meanwhile Davina, out walking, longing for money as always, feels "that events led nowhere, crisis was an illusion and that passions of momentary violent reality were struck off like sparks from the spirit, only to die" (62). In due course her aunt will die, and Davina will presumably inherit her money. What she will do with it and what will follow is already evident: from this hell is no escape.

"A Love Story 1939." The title of "A Love Story 1939" proves ironic. The loveless point, illustrated in variant ways, is that relationships that ought to provide the joys of shared companionship and love can be the source of misery for one or both parties. The mist covering the Irish seaside hotel on this out-of-season evening is the first indication of muddle. The presentation is very like a stage play. In turn, three different couples enact their scenes, the hotel manager and other members of the staff moving between them. Finally, several of the characters, involved in driving a local woman and her daughter home, come together. Only one of the six principals is remotely happy, but he is really caught up in a repetitious round as the woman with whom he is sharing a week at the hotel sadly understands. He is susceptible to all attractive young women, and in readily "loving" all of them he loves none of them. His charm is a form of curse. The most painful case involves the youngest couple: she, thirty-two, is wealthy, and he, twenty-four, whom she clearly loves, has allowed himself to be bought because he wants time and security in which to become a writer. She is a jealous keeper who exacts obedience, but receives in return the most grudging of responses, which provide her with a steady diet of anxiety. The story's grimest image shows him sitting alone in their expensive car slumped against the wheel, "a dying pig that has died" (172).

Remission

The stories so far considered display few instances of life's happier possibilities. From the writer's stance, of course, drama more readily resides in failure, disappointment, and disaster. While Elizabeth Bowen does have her light moments (chapter 1, for example, considered "The Working Party"), her propensity for exploring the workings of disenchantment and disorientation clearly reflect her sense of life in her times. The final four stories I consider, however, are more positive in presenting individuals who are capable of moments of joy and of saving insights, or who possess the awareness and flexibility that allow for a more meaningful degree of fulfillment than yet seen. Happiness, if this is not too strong a word for the positive moments these stories exhibit, is hedged in by qualifications, but then, only the unaware discount the terrible fragility of joy and of flesh. These four stories are among the author's finest and, for me, "Summer Night," is her best.

"Her Table Spread." Does "Her Table Spread" end with the possibility of redemption, or conclude with a wistful sadness of unfulfilled opportunity? This delightful concoction only hints at what may follow the closing words. That it does contain, however, a unique epiphany for the protagonist Alban is certain. This is another of Bowen's visiting stories. The young Londoner comes to the castle of Valeria Cuffe on the coast of Ireland, although he has "heard they were all mad." Valeria, single, wealthy, "of statuesque development" is, at twenty-five, "still detained in childhood" (84). The possibility of marriage is her motive for inviting Alban.

On his first evening at the castle, Alban is impressed by the elegance of the gowns and by the dinner table. He assumes he is the focus of attention, but he is soon disabused. In the estuary below a destroyer is anchored. Some months previous, at a time when Valeria was absent, a destroyer had likewise stopped over and the officers (including one named Garrett) came ashore to be entertained to dinner in a nearby home. Now Valeria, convinced that tonight officers will ascend to enjoy her hospitality, waits in anticipation. For her the destroyer is a fertile source of fantasy:

> When he and she were married (she inclined a little to Mr Garrett) they would invite all the Navy up the estuary and give them tea. Her estuary would be filled up, like a regatta, with loud excited battleships tooting to one another and flags flying. The terrace would be covered with grateful sailors, leaving room for the band. She would keep the peacocks her aunt did not allow. His friends would be surprised to notice that Mr Garrett had meanwhile become an admiral, all gold. He would lead the other admirals into the Castle and say, while they wiped their feet respectfully: "These are my wife's statues; she has given them to me. One is Mars, one is Mercury. We have a Venus, but she is not dressed. And wait till I show you our silver and gold plates . . ." The Navy would be unable to tear itself away (89).

Since no one comes up the hill through the pouring rain, Valeria excuses herself, fetches a lantern, and begins waving it from the brow. Old Mr. Rossiter, with Alban following, makes for the boathouse to stand guard. He is fearful she will come for a boat for "she's a fine oar." As the men have a whiskey sitting in the dark, Rossiter says, "It's time that girl was married, and observes that "she's a girl you could shape." Alban's attitude remains "negative." When he leaves Rossiter to climb the hill back to the castle he is mistaken for an officer. Valeria cries out to the others, "*Mr. Garrett has landed.*" Alban, looking up through the rain, sees the waiting women and hears Valeria laugh "like a princess, magnificently justified." For him it is a transcendent experience: "Their unseen faces were all three lovely, and, in the silence after the laughter, such a strong tenderness reached him that, standing there in full manhood, he was for a moment not exiled. For a moment, without moving or speaking, he stood, in the dark, in a flame, as though all three said: 'My darling . . .'" (92). Early the next morning, while the castle sleeps, the destroyer, fortuitously, steams away.

"Mysterious Kôr." "Mysterious Kôr" and the next story to be considered, "The Happy Autumn Fields," are from Elizabeth Bowen's most highly regarded story collection, *The Demon Lover and Other Stories*—works concerned with Londoners living through the blitz. In her postscript to the book, the author characterized it as "resistance writing" reflecting the situation where "one counteracts fear by fear, stress by stress." (The collection's title story has already been considered.) A crucial attribute of these stories is "hallucination," which Bowen characterizes as "an unconscious, instinctive, saving resort on the part of the characters: life, mechanized by the controls of wartime, and emotionally torn and impoverished by change, had to complete itself in *some* way." The next two stories, thus, have to do with "instinctive, saving resort."

The two young women in "Mysterious Kôr" each negotiate a metaphysical journey: the one from innocence to experience (disenchantment); the other, in Blakean terms, from experience to higher innocence. The ambience of the story's evening is potent. Though no German bombers are above, for obvious reasons, London is under assault from a full moon, so "moonlight drenched the city and searched it." For Pepita and her soldier boyfriend, Arthur, walking the streets, the city is "unreal" and the light "perhaps more than the senses and nerves could bear" (146). Pepita is frustrated. She and Arthur walk because they have no other place in which to be alone. Eventually Pepita will take Arthur back to the flat she shares with Callie where he will spend the night. When she and Arthur finally return to the flat Pepita knows Callie will be waiting with cocoa and chat after which they will turn in and "that would be that, and that would be all." Of the three characters, Pepita most feels the pressure of circumstances. What she has been doing increasingly is spending more and more of her waking hours inhabiting the deserted city of Kôr, which she has remembered from her youthful reading. It has become for her a retreat of quiet order countering the densely packed chaos of London. She tells Arthur of this in wishing they were there together and explains her logic: "If you can blow whole places out of existence, you can blow whole places into it" (149).

Pepita's response to circumstances, her suprareality, stands in contrast to Callie's romanticism. This "physically shy . . . brotherless virgin" is, unknowingly, at risk. Thinking the moonlight wonderful for the lovers she is "content with reflecting the heat of love." Her innocence is manifest when, as she and Pepita climb into bed, she asks, "Do you think Arthur's got all he wants?" Yet this is a night of inner illumination for Callie, and for Arthur as well. He comes to see that Pepita is not his type and that he is able to gain more insight into Callie than he can manage with Pepita. Callie's middle-of-the-night chat with him, while Pepita sleeps, brings about her release from innocence. As she opens a window, Arthur asks, "And how's your moon?" By now it has dimmed and, "To Callie it seemed likely there would never be such a moon again; and on the whole she thought this was for the best" (161). Back in bed Callie places her recognition of the relationship between moonlight and romance into a larger context: "The loss of her own mysterious expectations of her love for love, was a small thing beside the war's total of unlived lives." Beside her Pepita dreams of both Arthur and Kôr, but in the end "it was to Kôr's finality that she turned." In one way or another the remarkable human mind finds ways of defusing what threatens it.

"The Happy Autumn Fields." "The Happy Autumn Fields" is something of a twilight zone story. The surprise shift more than a third of the way into the story attests to the intensity of Mary's imaginative experience. Here, in place of Pepita's Kôr, is a domestic drama in late Victorian Ireland. The vividly realized re-creation has been set off by the old letters Mary has been going through in her bomb-damaged house. That she has been cauterized by the bombing is clear when she tells Travis, "We only know inconvenience now, not sorrow." The fantasy—set in what is probably Bowen's Court—is intuitively theurapeutic. Mary's appeal to Travis for another two hours in which to pursue her narrative indicates her need to sustain the swelling emotional flow (and also makes her a surrogate for the creative author). His discrete removal of the letters as he leaves proves crucial to Mary's later acquisition of truth about her "history." However idyllic seeming this reconstruction initially appears, its essential lesson is that threat, loss, pain and death attend life at all times.

The relationship of Sarah and her younger sister Henrietta appears abnormally intense. Sarah thinks, "Rather than they should cease to lie in the same bed she prayed they might lie in the same grave" (250). Eugene, brother Fitzgeorge's friend, with his eyes on Sarah, threatens to come between them as he does when he dismounts from his horse to walk with them across the fields. Since the sisters virtually think and feel alike, Sarah registers Henrietta's pain, yet, Henrietta is no sentimentalist: "It has always been she who with one fierce act destroyed any toy that might be outgrown." Later, when Eugene is taking his leave from his visit, Henrietta says, "Whatever tries to come between me and Sarah becomes nothing." At this point Mary's mind is brought sharply back to the present because a nearby explosion rocks the house.

Later, to the returned Travis, who finds her crying, she says she is "left with a fragment torn out of a day," yet, emotionally, she is settled, "drained by a dream" (265). Having read the letters in the interim, Travis casts further light on the scant hints out of which she has fashioned her emotional scenario. Eugene, riding away from the house after a visit one night, is thrown from his horse and killed. Fitzgeorge, in one of his letters, expresses puzzlement as to why the horse would shy "in those empty fields." Neither Sarah nor Henrietta ever married and both, seemingly, died young. Mary, both emotionally and aesthetically, is free to quit her unsafe house with Travis.

"Summer Night." Published in 1941, "Summer Night" anticipates *The Demon Lover* stories both because of its World War II context and its characters who, though living in southern Ireland, reflect the war's pressures. It also foreshadows *The Heat of the Day* by substantiating a statement made by one of that novel's characters: "War, if you come to think of it, hasn't started anything that wasn't there already." No brief summary of this novella, the author's finest short work, can do justice to its reverberating suggestiveness.

Ostensibly off to spend the night with relatives, Emma, on this lovely Saturday evening, drives cross country for her first assignation. At home are her husband, the Major, two young daughters, and the aging Aunt Fran who lives with them. Waiting ahead is Robinson, married but separated, who is entertaining unexpected visitors, a neighboring lady and her holidaying brother. Meanwhile a murderous air battle is taking place over southern England. The leisurely cutting back and forth between the travelling and arriving Emma, scenes at the family home, and at Robinson's, belies the mounting tension registered by several of the characters. The total impression of the work is that somehow all of life has been touched upon. As Victoria Glendinning sagely observes, "the resonances and implications it leaves behind it go so far beyond its relatively restrained narrative."[8] Ranging across a broad spectrum of themes and raising several provocative questions, the work sustains a poised and witty ambivalence.

The narrative culminates when Emma and Robinson are finally alone. Robinson, an unintellectual factory manager who drives a high-powered car and is viewed as something of a bluebeard by the local women, possesses an "imperturbable male personality." Emma arrives in an exulted mood, but Robinson's experienced and businesslike manner quickly dampens it. What began as her "pilgrimage" is reduced to an "adventure." She realizes she is "being settled down to as calmly as he might settle down to a meal." For her it is a crisis that, as they walk and talk in his garden, she finds she can handle:

"she thought for a minute he had broken her heart, and she knew now he had broken her fairytale" (130).

Unaware of Emma's feelings, Robinson is equally oblivious to the strong response he has prompted in his earlier visitor, Justin, who in his intellectualism and homosexuality is Robinson's antithesis. Justin's usual practice of breaking "his monkish life in the city" with a continental holiday has had to be replaced because of the war with a return home to visit his deaf sister Queenie. Unlike Emma, Justin cannot swallow his feelings. Depressed by the war and unsettled by Robinson, he is drawn "like a perverse person in love, to expose all his own piques, crotchets and weaknesses." Sounding very much like Rupert Birkin addressing Gerald Critch in Lawrence's *Women in Love*, he seeks to share his belief in the need for new modes of thinking and feeling. Later, back in his hotel room and still wrought up, he cannot foreswear writing Robinson, although fully aware of the "indifference" that will greet his explanations and farewell.

Queenie, in her quiet private world, and Robinson, who tells Justin he wants to enjoy himself in his little free time, are the only ones who seem content with themselves and appear impervious to the wartime tensions. As such, are they betrayers of the civilized world or a saving remnant? Seeing them together, Justin thinks, "They are both against me. . . . She does not hear with her ears, he does not hear with his mind."

The Major is a kindly, unimaginative man deeply troubled by the war and his own inability to become involved. He is oblivious to his wife's emotional needs. As he locks up the house thinking all is well, his wife is cuckolding him, and his youngest daughter, Vivie, unable to sleep, is rising from her bed. She removes her nightgown and races about naked. Instinctively registering the anarchy in the air, she chalks "her chest, belly and thighs with stars and snakes, red, yellow and blue" and dances upon her parent's bed.

Aunt Fran's eventual confrontation with and reaction to Vivie parodies Marlow registering the horror of Kurtz. She is made aware of "the enemy within" and thinks, "Each moment is everywhere, it holds the war in its crystal; there is no elsewhere, no other place" (123). Perhaps there is one. At the close, Queenie drifts into sleep smiling, reliving an experience from twenty years previous when she led a young man through leaf tunnels to the edge of a lake. Tonight the man she has by the hand is Robinson. Instinctively she knows that life's only certainty resides in the imagination. Her silent sustaining paradisal tranquility stands in the midst of humanity's restless sea.

Chapter Six

Bowen and the Critics

Elizabeth Bowen's critical environment becomes richer with the passing years. Since Jocelyn Brooke published his British Council monograph on her in 1952, Bowen has never lacked for serious critics. But as William Heath pointed out in *Elizabeth Bowen: An Introduction to Her Novels*, she was rather unfortunate in her earliest critics because "her achievement has been least understood by those who have admired it most extravagantly."[1] By demonstrating "the toughness inherent in her intellect and essential to her art," Heath laid the foundation for serious contemplation of her work. Though Bowen published two novels after Heath produced his study, it remains one of the most detailed and sophisticated of considerations.

After publication of my original (1971) version of this study came Edwin J. Kenney, Jr.'s sound if brief *Elizabeth Bowen*, which bypasses three of the early novels to concentrate on the remainder. Bowen studies were greatly enhanced in 1977 when Victoria Glendinning published her full-scale biography. This has provided an enriched context for the reading of Bowen's work. Patricia Craig contributed a shorter but lively biography to Penguin's "Lives of Modern Women" series in 1986. Undoubtedly the finest and fullest study of the work is Hermoine Lee's *Elizabeth Bowen: An Estimation* (1981). In addition to the novels and an ample sampling of the short stories, this study examines a considerable portion of the author's vast output of nonfiction: the reviews, articles, introductions, and radio talks. Hermoine Lee is especially concerned to show how Bowen grows out of and continues a rich tradition of Anglo-Irish writing. In addition to these books, of course, can be compiled an extensive bibliography of articles and chapters in books on various Bowen fiction.

The preponderance of this criticism, inevitably, is laudatory, and when otherwise the critic is generally concerned with one of Bowen's weaker works.[2] Certainly the Bowen critics agree that she is an uneven writer. In a sense this is one indication of her worth: she was prepared to try different tacks and to take risks. In any event, the varying estimates of her individual works presents an interesting facet of Bowen criticism and prompts this brief survey of judgments.

It comes as no surprise to anyone in some degree familiar with Bowen's fiction that *The Death of the Heart* is considered her finest novel. Kenney is representative in observing, "This work is the culmination of Elizabeth Bowen's treatment of the theme of youthful innocence confronting the risks of life in a world of unsympathetic, 'fallen' adults, the finest of her novels, and a significant achievement in modern fiction."[3] Hermoine Lee suggests the novel merits "as much attention as has been given to *Mrs. Dalloway*, or *Brideshead Revisited*, or *The End of the Affair*."[4] John Mellors is a rarity in expressing a reservation: "Yet even *The Death of the Heart* has its *longueurs*, stretches in which we seem to be reading an essayist rather than a novelist."[5]

There is also considerable unanimity about what constitutes the weakest work. *The Hotel*, the first of the novels, is usually viewed as apprenticework and most interesting as a foretelling of things to come. Both *Friends and Relations* and *A World of Love* have nominations as the least effective of the books, though Victoria Glendinning includes the latter among the novels she would select as "essential to illustrate both the quality of her writing and its development."[7] Though neither *To the North* or *The Little Girls* draw high ratings, both have their advocates. Mellors places *To the North* with *The Death of the Heart* as among her best novels. It is, in his view, "an enchanting novel with a believable plot which does not make the wrong demands on the characters who act it out."[8] Kenney regards *The Little Girls* as Bowen's "wittiest and funniest novels," but Sullivan believes *The Little Girls* and *Eva Trout* "were *tours de force* which did not succeed."[9] Glendinning admires *Eva Trout*, and Kenney, while acknowledging the adverse criticism it has prompted, undertakes to counter it.[10]

The remaining three novels enjoy the highest general regard after *The Death of the Heart*. It is easy to agree with Kenney that *The Last September* is the author's "first important novel" and perhaps even Sullivan's escalation of this into her first "major" novel."[11] Heath characterizes it as "one of her most complex novels, rich . . . in ambiguities left for the reader to explore."[12] It was the author's own personal favorite quite likely because much of her own youth is reflected in the thoughts and desires of the heroine Lois.[13]

Which novel is Bowen's second best? This is the most contentious issue in Bowen studies, as most critics divide between *The House in Paris* and *The Heat of the Day*. For Frederick Karl, *The House in Paris* is an important novel and Sullivan thinks it "almost as fine as *The Death of the Heart*."[14] While recognizing the undoubted merits of the work, other critics enter caveats. Heath feels the lack of attention paid "Leopold's consciousness" is a weakness, and Kenney sees it, finally, as "disjointed."[15] I think the characterization of Henrietta is one of the highlights of Bowen's work, but I am troubled by the suicide of Max, which comes across as too pat a plot solution. A similar mix of the favorable and the reserved characterizes responses to *The Heat of the Day*. It is properly adjudged Bowen's most ambitious novel and her one attempt at the big work. Kenney and Heath both place it just below *The Death of the Heart*, as I do myself.[16]

A new note has been creeping into Bowen criticism that concerns the shorter fiction. Victoria Glendinning wonders if, in the future, it will appear to be the most highly regarded work:

> She made the short story particularly her own. In the stories—which were, she said, "a matter of vision rather than feeling"—she achieved a mastery that gives the best of them a perfection and unity that the sustained narrative and shifting emphases of a novel do not attempt. It may be that posterity will judge the best of her stories over her novels. . . .[17]

Mellors has no doubt whatever that the author is most impressive in her chief stories, the best of which he terms, "brilliantly successful."[18] His advocacy of the shorter work certainly accounts for his general coolness to the novels as a whole. He is especially impressed by the stories in *The Demon Lover* because it was "Bowen's unique achievement" to depict aspects of the wartime situation and mood as did no other writer and "then transform her findings into works of art." He believes the stories should outlast the novels.

Hermoine Lee thinks several of the stories are "outstanding . . . and can rival short stories as disparate as those of Katharine Mansfield, Rudyard Kipling, or M. R. James."[19] This is her personal list of the best: "Summer Night," "Her Table Spread," "A Love Story," "The Happy Autumn Fields," "The Disinherited," "The Cat Jumps," "Ivy Gripped the Steps," "The Demon Lover," and "Mysterious Kôr." I concur with this selection, but, along with Victoria Glendinning, add to it "A Day in the Dark."

In these stories and in *The Death of the Heart*, Elizabeth Bowen's gifts are at their zenith. These are works about which one feels no reservations because of the perfect melding of concern and artistry. They are totally achieved. About *The Last September* and *To the North* there is a similar degree of perfection, but in spite of this these novels do not carry the weight of *The House in Paris* and *The Heat of the Day*, two works that for all their many strengths contain elements not fully absorbed into their being. This is to judge by the highest of standards, for the truth is that Elizabeth Bowen is never other than interesting in even her lesser efforts. Certainly her successes mark her as one of the most notable of twentieth-century British writers. She is an author who enhances all of her readers.

Notes and References

Chapter One

1. *Bowen's Court*, (New York: Alfred A. Knopf, 1942), 4.

2. Preface to *Early Stories* (a re-edition of *Encounters*) (New York: Alfred A. Knopf, 1950), iii.

3. C. M. Bowra, *Memories, 1898–1939* (London: Weidenfeld and Nicholson, 1966), 190–91.

4. Victoria Glendinning, *Elizabeth Bowen* (London: Penguin, 1985), 23.

5. *Afterthought* (London: Longmans, Green, 1962), 209.

6. *Collected Impressions* (New York: Alfred A. Knopf, 1950), 67.

7. Preface to *Stories by Elizabeth Bowen* (New York: Alfred A. Knopf, 1959), v.

8. "The Working Party," in *Joining Charles* (New York: Alfred A. Knopf, 1929), 121.

9. *Collected Impressions*, 197.

10. Robert Frost, "The Oven Bird."

11. Glendinning, *Elizabeth Bowen*, 32.

12. Preface to *A Day in the Dark and Other Stories* (London: Jonathan Cape, 1965), 8.

13. W. H. Auden, "As I Walked Out One Evening," and "Lullaby."

14. Walter Allan, *Tradition and Dream* (London: Phoenix House, 1964), 191–92.

15. *The Heat of the Day* (New York: Alfred A. Knopf, 1948), 11.

16. *A Day in the Dark*, 8.

17. "The Disinherited," in *Stories by Elizabeth Bowen*, 47.

18. This is amplified in the preface to *A Day in the Dark*, 8.

19. *A Day in the Dark*, 9.

20. *Afterthought*, 152–3.

21. *Afterthought*, 208–9.

22. *The Death of the Heart* (London: Cape Collected Edition, 1948), 111.

23. *To the North* (London: Cape Collected Edition, 1952), 58–59.

Chapter Two

1. *The Hotel* (New York: Dial Press, 1927), 266; cited hereafter in the text by page number.

2. *The Last September* (New York: Alfred A. Knopf, 1952), 136; cited hereafter in the text by page number.

3. Hermoine Lee, *Elizabeth Bowen: An Estimation* (London: Vision/Barnes & Noble, 1981), 49)

Chapter Three

1. James Hall, *The Lunatic Giant in the Drawing Room* (Bloomington: Indiana University Press, 1968), 49.
2. *Friends and Relations* (New York: Dial Press), 21; cited hereafter in the text by page number.
3. *The House in Paris* (New York: Alfred A. Knopf, 1935), 69; cited hereafter in the text by page number.

Chapter Four

1. William Heath, *Elizabeth Bowen: An Introduction to Her Novels* (Madison: University of Wisconsin Press, 1961), 120.
2. *A World of Love* (New York: Alfred A. Knopf, 1955), 9; cited hereafter in the text by page number.
3. *The Little Girls* (New York: Alfred A. Knopf, 1964), 188; cited hereafter in the text by page number.
4. This allusion may seem less fanciful when it is noted that later in the novel Dinah says "in the voice of one continuing aloud a train of thought: 'You huffed and you puffed and you blew my house down'" (244).
5. *Eva Trout* (New York: Alfred A. Knopf, 1969), 133; cited hereafter in the text by page number.

Chapter Five

1. *Stories by Elizabeth Bowen*, x.
2. The quotations in this section are from the prefaces of either *Stories by Elizabeth Bowen* or *A Day in the Dark*.
3. *A Day in the Dark*, 276; cited hereafter in the text by page number.
4. "Foothold," in *Joining Charles*, 149.
5. "The Queer Heart," in *Look at All Those Roses* (London: Victor Gollancz, 1941), 151.
6. Glendinning, *Elizabeth Bowen*, 93.
7. Patricia Craig, *Elizabeth Bowen* (London: Penguin, 1986), 76.
8. Glendinning, *Elizabeth Bowen*, 112.

Chapter Six

1. Heath, *Elizabeth Bowen*, 152.
2. A prime instance is Geoffrey Wagner's "Elizabeth Bowen and the Artificial Novel," *Essays in Criticism* 13 (1963): 155–63, which considers *A World of Love*.

3. Edwin Kenney, Jr., *Elizabeth Bowen* (Lewisburg, Pa.: Bucknell University Press, 1975), 53.

4. Hermoine Lee, *Elizabeth Bowen: An Estimate*, 11.

5. John Mellors, "Dreams in War: Second Thoughts on Elizabeth Bowen," *London Magazine* 19 (1979): 67.

6. Glendinning, *Elizabeth Bowen*, 125.

7. Ibid., 1.

8. Mellors, "Dreams in War," 88.

9. Kenney, *Elizabeth Bowen*, 86; Walter Sullivan, "A Sense of Place: Elizabeth Bowen and the Landscape of the Heart," *Sewanee Review* 84 (1976): 142–49.

10. Glendinning, *Elizabeth Bowen*, 227; Kenney, *Elizabeth Bowen*, 104.

11. Kenney, *Elizabeth Bowen*, 31; Sullivan, "A Sense of Place," 144.

12. Heath, *Elizabeth Bowen*, 32.

13. See Glendinning, *Elizabeth Bowen*, 68.

14. Frederick Karl, *The Contemporary English Novel* (New York: Farrar, Straus and Cudahy, 1962), 115; Sullivan, "A Sense of Place," 146.

15. Heath, *Elizabeth Bowen*, 148; Kenney, *Elizabeth Bowen*, 53.

16. Kenney, *Elizabeth Bowen*, 65; Heath, *Elizabeth Bowen*, 70.

17. Glendinning, *Elizabeth Bowen*, 1.

18. Mellors, "Dreams in War," 65.

19. Lee, *Elizabeth Bowen*, 11.

Selected Bibliography

PRIMARY SOURCES

Novels and Stories (in order of publication)

Encounters. London: Sidgwick and Jackson, 1923. Fourteen short stories (republished, along with *Ann Lee's,* in *Early Stories*, New York: Alfred A. Knopf, 1950): "Breakfast," "Daffodils," "The Return," "The Confidante," "Requiescat," "All Saints," "The New House," "Lunch," "The Lover," "Mrs. Windermere," "The Shadowy Third," "The Evil That Men Do—," "Sunday Evening," "Coming Home."

Ann Lee's and Other Stories. London: Sidgwick and Jackson, 1926. Eleven short stories (republished, along with *Encounters*, in *Early Stories*, New York: Alfred A. Knopf, 1950): "Ann Lee's," "The Parrot," "The Visitor," "The Contessina," "Human Habitation," "The Secession," "Making Arrangements," "The Storm," "Charity," "The Back Drawing-Room," "Recent Photograph."

The Hotel. London: Constable, 1927. Republished in Cape Collected Edition, 1950.

Joining Charles. London: Constable, 1929. Republished in Cape Collected Edition, 1952. Eleven short stories: "Joining Charles," "The Jungle," "Shoes: An International Episode," "The Dancing-Mistress," "Aunt Tatty," "Dead Mabelle," "The Working Party," "Foothold," "The Cassowary," "Telling," "Mrs. Moysey."

The Last September. London: Constable, 1929. Republished in Cape Collected Edition, 1948.

Friends and Relations. London: Constable, 1931. Republished in Cape Collected Edition, 1951.

To the North. London: Victor Gollancz, 1932. Republished in Cape Collected Edition, 1952.

The Cat Jumps. London: Victor Gollancz, 1934. Republished in Cape Collected Edition, 1949. Twelve short stories: "The Tommy Crans," "The Good Girls," "The Cat Jumps," "The Last Night in the Old Home," "The Disinherited," "Maria," "Her Table Spread," "The Little Girl's Room," "Firelight in the Flat," "The Man of the Family," "The Needlecase," "The Apple-Tree."

The House in Paris. London: Victor Gollancz, 1935. Republished in Cape Collected Edition, 1949.

The Death of the Heart. London: Victor Gollancz, 1938. Republished in Cape Collected Edition, 1948.

Look at All Those Roses. London: Victor Gollancz, 1941. Republished in Cape Collected Edition, 1951. Fourteen short stories: "Reduced," "Tears, Idle Tears," "A Walk in the Woods," "A Love Story," "Look at All Those Roses," "Attractive

Modern Homes," "The Easter Egg Party," "Love," "No. 16," "A Queer Heart," "The Girl with the Stoop," "Unwelcome Idea," "Oh, Madam . . . ," "Summer Night."

The Demon Lover. London: Jonathan Cape, 1945. Published as *Ivy Gripped the Steps* in New York: Alfred A. Knopf, 1946. Republished in Cape Collected Edition, 1952. Twelve short stories: "In the Square," "Sunday Afternoon," "The Inherited Clock," "The Cherry Soul," "Songs My Father Sang Me," "The Demon Lover," "Careless Talk," "The Happy Autumn Fields," "Ivy Gripped the Steps," "Pink May," "Green Holly," "Mysterious Kôr."

The Heat of the Day. London: Jonathan Cape, 1949. Republished in Cape Collected Edition, 1954.

A World of Love. London: Jonathan Cape, 1955.

Stories by Elizabeth Bowen. New York: Alfred A. Knopf, 1959. The author's personal selection of eighteen stories, with a preface: "Coming Home," "The Storm," "The Tommy Crans," "Her Table Spread," "The Disinherited," "The Easter Egg Party," "No. 16," "Reduced," "Look at All Those Roses," "A Love Story," "Summer Night," "Songs My Father Sang Me," "The Inherited Clock," "Sunday Afternoon," "The Demon Lover," "Ivy Gripped the Steps," "The Happy Autumn Fields," "Mysterious Kôr."

The Little Girls. London: Jonathan Cape, 1964.

A Day in the Dark and Other Stories. London: Jonathan Cape, 1965. Twenty short stories: "A Day in the Dark," "The Disinherited," "Breakfast," "Reduced," "Her Table Spread," "I Hear You Say So," "Summer Night," "Gone Away," "Mysterious Kôr," "A Love Story," "The Dancing-Mistress," "Look at All Those Roses," "Hand in Glove," "The Demon Lover," "No. 16," "The Cheery Soul," "The Happy Autumn Fields," "The Dolt's Tale," "The Cat Jumps," "Ivy Gripped the Steps."

Eva Trout. London, Jonathan Cape, 1969.

Nonfiction (in order of publication)

Bowen's Court. London: Longmans, Green, 1942. History of the Bowen family and its home.

Seven Winters. London: Longmans, Green, 1942. Brief autobiography.

English Novelists. London: Collins, 1946. Short literary history.

Collected Impressions. London: Longmans, Green, 1950. Consists of essays, prefaces, and reviews.

The Shelbourne: A Center of Dublin Life for More Than a Century. London: George G. Harrap, 1951. Social history.

A Time in Rome. New York: Alfred A. Knopf, 1960. Recounts seven months spent in Rome.

Afterthought. Pieces about Writing. London: Longmans, Green, 1962. Comprises broadcasts, prefaces, reflective sketches, reviews, and travel pieces.

Play

Castle Anna. A play, coauthored by John Perry. Unpublished. First performed in London in March 1948.

SECONDARY SOURCES

Books

Allen, Walter. *Tradition and Dream. A Critical Survey of British and American Fiction from the 1920s to the Present Day.* London: Phoenix House, 1964. Comments are succinct but apt.

Brooke, Jocelyn. *Elizabeth Bowen.* London: Longmans, Green for the British Council, 1952. This pioneering work is chiefly an appreciation.

Craig, Patricia. *Elizabeth Bowen.* London: Penguin, 1986. Part of the Penguin "Lives of Modern Women" series, this biography, compared with the Glendinning book, is a brief life, but the style is lively.

Fraser, G. S. *The Modern Writer and His World.* London: Derek Verschoyle, 1953. Helpfully places Elizabeth Bowen among her contemporaries.

Glendinning, Victoria. *Elizabeth Bowen.* London: Wiedenfeld & Nicolson, 1977; published by Penguin Books in 1985 in their "Penguin Literary Biographies" series. An excellent biography and likely to remain the definitive one.

Hall, James. *The Lunatic Giant in the Drawing Room: The British and American Novel since 1930.* Bloomington: Indiana University Press, 1968. The chapter on Elizabeth Bowen contains a superior analysis of *The Death of the Heart.*

Heath, William. *Elizabeth Bowen: An Introduction to Her Novels.* Madison: University of Wisconsin Press, 1961. Every serious student of Elizabeth Bowen ought to read this sophisticated study even though it appeared before publication of her concluding novels.

Karl, Frederick. *The Contemporary English Novel.* New York: Farrar, Straus and Cudahy, 1962. A chapter entitled, "The World of Elizabeth Bowen," discusses several of her novels in a reasonable if somewhat adverse manner.

Kenney, Jr., Edwin. *Elizabeth Bowen.* Lewisburg: Bucknell University Press, 1975. Brief and selective, but perceptive.

Lee, Hermoine. *Elizabeth Bowen: An Estimation.* London: Vision/Barnes & Noble, 1981. Without question, the most detailed and valuable book available on the work.

O'Faolin, Sean. *The Vanishing Hero: Studies in the Novelists of the Twenties.* London: Eyre and Spottiswood, 1956. The chapter on Elizabeth Bowen discusses only the earlier novels but is sound.

Articles

Davenport, Gary. "Elizabeth Bowen and the Big House," *Southern Humanities Review* 8 (1974):27–34. Discusses the tradition of the big house underlying *The Last September.*

Darenkamp, Angela G. "'Fallon Leap': Bowen's *The Heat of the Day*," *Critique* 10 (1968):13–21. Explores the tensions centered in imagery and language.

Franstino, Daniel V. "Elizabeth Bowen's 'The Demon Lover': Psychosis or Seduction?" *Studies in Short Fiction* 17 (1980):483–87. Considers the story's similarities to the ballad of the same title.

Greene, George. "Elizabeth Bowen: Imagination as Therapy," *Perspective* 14 (1965):42–52. Cordial consideration of the four novels preceding *Eva Trout.* Especially illuminating on *The Little Girls.*

Heinemann, Alison. "The Indoor Landscape in Bowen's *The Death of the Heart*," *Critique* 10 (1968):5–12. Discloses the emotional importance of objects in the novel.

Hooper, Brad. "Elizabeth Bowen's 'The Happy Autumn Fields': A Dream or Not?" *Studies in Short Fiction* 21 (1984):151–53. Argues for the proximate nature of the story's two realities.

Hughes, Douglas A. "Cracks in the Psyche: Elizabeth Bowen's 'The Demon Lover,'" *Studies in Short Fiction* 10 (1973):411–13. A psychological reading of the story.

Mellors, John. "Dreams in War: Second Thoughts on Elizabeth Bowen," *London Magazine* 19 (1979):64–69. Gives reasons for regarding the better stories as Elizabeth Bowen's best work.

Mitchell, Edward. "Themes in Elizabeth Bowen's Short Stories," *Critique* 8 (1966):41–54. Interesting as the first effort to categorize the stories through basic thematic patterns.

Rupp, Richard Henry. "The Post-War Fiction of Elizabeth Bowen," *Xavier University Studies* 4 (1965):55–67. Seeks to account for the perceived decline following *The Death of the Heart.*

Saul, George Brandon. "The Short Stories of Elizabeth Bowen," *Arizona Quarterly* 21 (1965):53–59. Judges Elizabeth Bowen's success in the genre to be intermittent rather than developmental.

Sharp, Sister M. Corona, O.S.U. "The House as Setting and Symbol in Three Novels by Elizabeth Bowen," *Xavier University Studies* 2 (1963):93–103. The novels are *The Last September*, *The House In Paris*, and *The Death of the Heart.*

Sullivan, Walter. "A Sense of Place: Elizabeth Bowen and the Landscape of the Heart," *Sewanee Review* 84 (1976):142–49. Though brief, a thoughtful and warm overview of her career.

Van Duyn, Mona. "Pattern and Pilgrimage: A Reading of *The Death of the Heart*," *Critique* 4 (1961):52–66. A telling illumination of the novels' subtlety and complexity.

Index